Rebooting
American Politics

Rebooting American Politics

The Internet Revolution

JASON GAINOUS AND KEVIN M. WAGNER

ROWMAN & LITTLEFIELD PUBLISHERS, INC.
Lanham • Boulder • New York • Toronto • Plymouth, UK

Published by Rowman & Littlefield Publishers, Inc.
A wholly owned subsidiary of The Rowman & Littlefield Publishing Group, Inc.
4501 Forbes Boulevard, Suite 200, Lanham, Maryland 20706
http://www.rowmanlittlefield.com

Estover Road, Plymouth PL6 7PY, United Kingdom

British Library Cataloguing in Publication Information Available

Library of Congress Cataloging-in-Publication Data
Gainous, Jason, 1971–
    Rebooting American politics: The Internet revolution / Jason Gainous and Kevin M.
Wagner.
        p. cm.
    Includes bibliographical references and index.
    ISBN 978-1-4422-1049-3 (cloth : alk. paper)
    ISBN 978-1-4422-1050-9 (pbk. : alk. paper)
    ISBN 978-1-4422-1051-6 (e-book)
    1. Internet—Political aspects—United States. 2. Political participation—United
States—Computer network resources. I. Wagner, Kevin M., 1971– II. Title.
    JK468.A8G34 2011
    324.0973—dc22
                                                                    2010051418

Printed in the United States of America

I would like to dedicate this book to my grandfather, Kenneth Webber. My work is greatly improved as a result of his tireless editing efforts. And without the love of my wife, Sherry, and daughter, Bella, there would be no book, for I would be lost.

—JG

This work is dedicated to my wife, Jodie, whose love and tireless support have made this journey possible, and to my children, Madeleine and Alexander, who make the future seem so bright.

—KW

Contents

Figures

Acknowledgments

Each author contributed equally to this book. They are listed alphabetically. We would like to thank all of the students in Jason Gainous's Internet and Politics class for their useful comments. In particular, we offer our thanks to Sarah E. Hackman, Jessica Logsdon, and Shane T. Shaughnessy. Additionally, we would like to thank Adam David Marlowe for his help with this project. We would like to thank the *American Review of Politics* for allowing us to reprint a revised version of our 2007 article, "The Electronic Ballot Box: Class, Age and Racial Bias on the Internet" (chapter 4). We would also like to thank *The Journal of Legislative Studies* for allowing us to reprint a revised version of a 2010 article (chapter 8). This article has previously been published in *The Journal of Legislative Studies* © 2010 copyright Taylor & Francis; *The Journal of Legislative Studies* is available online at: http://www.informaworld.com/smpp/content~db=all~content=a916687888~frm=titlelink.

1

Evolution, Revolution, and the Internet

This book is about the Internet and provides an examination of some, though not all, of the ways the Internet is changing the face of American politics. While the Internet is the instrument being examined, the book is less a study of technology and much more a focus on the power of society and government to adapt. At its essence, this book is about change. It is about fundamental change in the way we interact with each other and ultimately how we choose to govern ourselves. In this study, the Internet is the stimulus for the change; it provides the mechanism by which people and society can alter their behaviors and create a different relationship with each other.

Nonetheless, this book is less about mechanisms and more about people. It examines the implications of a technology shift which we contend is so momentous that the very connections which form and structure our society are likely to change and reform in ways we are now just beginning to observe, with implications we can only estimate. To do this, we will examine why the Internet presents such a significant change in the very structure and operation of our society and governance. We will examine what it means to be a politician and a voter in an age of instant communication on an often uncontrollable, interactive, multifaceted, evolving network. We will examine how grassroots activism, supporter outreach, fundraising, campaigning, and even basic communication are changing, and are likely to change further, in the Internet era. These are not necessarily novel areas of examination but our methodological approach confronts them in a way that offers, perhaps, more generalizable results than much of the previous work focused on similar topics. We present a theoretical approach to understanding the changes produced by the Internet along with empirical evidence as support. This book will be among the first literature in the field to step beyond assumption and conjecture to look at actual measures of Internet impact. Much of the research on the influence of the Internet on American politics is speculative rather than empirical, and when it is empirical, it is primarily descriptive as opposed to inferential. While some of the scholarship has attempted to put actual measures to the Internet's role in politics, the scope is often limited. In this book, we expand the field and directly address a broader and more comprehensive array of subjects in American politics. This book seeks to bridge the divide between supposition and evidence, and by so doing, provide a foundation for future research and study of the Internet in American politics.

In each chapter we examine some of the implications of the Internet and measure the expectations against the reality. Does the Internet stimulate an expansion in political knowledge in the electorate? Does the Internet as a means of voting create equity or inequity? Does online social networking encourage and stimulate participation and replace more traditional methods of political engagement? Does Internet campaigning work? Is the nature of Internet communication with its vast and ever-growing size having a polarizing effect on the electorate? And if so, what are the implications? We also tackle the much-considered but only partially-understood area of Internet fundraising and consider the democratizing effect of expanding the number of sources of campaign money. Yet before we do any of these things, we need to begin with the Internet itself.

While shrouded by the discussions of both science and philosophy, Internet technology is fairly simple to understand. The United States Supreme Court has defined the term *Internet* fairly directly as an international network of interconnected computers (*Reno v. ACLU* 1997). Former Alaska senator Ted Stevens simplified it as "a series of tubes" though that particular description was a misunderstanding concerning how computers link with each other (Singel and Poulsen 2006). Nonetheless, the basic construct of joined interconnected communication stations is largely accurate if not particularly descriptive or suggestive of larger implications. What differentiates the Internet and makes it unique as a means to convey information is its decentralized nature. No state or industry controls the content of the Internet. It is a network of networks that links literally hundreds of millions of devices around the globe, largely outside the traditional networks of communication.[1]

The network protocols allow transmissions to be broken into packets and sent virtually anywhere using a remarkably fast yet unpredictable and varied route. The route itself is irrelevant, and the nature of the data transmitted can be virtually any content in multiple formats. Network protocols are open and published, so it is difficult, though not impossible, at least in the short term, for any actor to control the Internet. China, and more recently Iran, has had some success in limiting content using filters. Yet, there continue to be ways around such filters such as proxies and encryption (Chadwick 2006).

Ironically, attempts at predicting longer-term implications of the Internet and its progeny were regularly confined to speculative fiction. The term *cyberspace* (a portmanteau of cybernetics and space) originated in a science fiction story by William Gibson. The Canadian science fiction writer first coined the term in his novelette "Burning Chrome," though the word did not become popularized until he used it again in the novel *Neuromancer* (Gibson 1985). Gibson's view is a wary look at the dehumanizing impact of inexpensive and ubiquitous technology. Nonetheless, in modern jargon, cyberspace has a generally positive connotation and is used to describe virtually anything that exists largely within the computing network known as the Internet (Allison 2002; Klotz 2004). Anything that occurs or takes place within this computer network is referred to as having occurred in cyberspace.

The impact of speculative fiction has forced empirical assessments of the impact of technology to be more judicious in their assumptions to avoid overly exuberant predictions with little foundation. This is especially true in an academic environment where the implications of technological change are harder to understand in the context of traditional historic events. In some ways the changes from the growth and penetration of the Internet are easy to underestimate, as the important critical shifts throughout history are often accompanied or perhaps marked by violence or more measurable and tangible events. The shifts fostered by the Internet sit well outside this paradigm. The change the Internet produces in American politics is not the kind of change that leaves scars on the landscape or even pages of interpretation in legal volumes. The government is not being overthrown, no protesters are marching on Washington, no new constitution is being written.

In the absence of the more physical markers of change, scholars fall into largely two camps when considering the implications of the Internet on politics. Some propose that the Internet will provide the means by which people and politicians can expand the otherwise limited political field, creating more opportunities for ideas and candidates (Barber 2001; Corrado and Firestone 1996; Hagen and Mayer 2000; Rash 1997). In this view, the Internet is a positive democratizing entity that helps remove the barriers that favor some groups and individuals in the electorate. This projection is generally called the equalization theory (Barber 2001).

Alternatively, some have contended that the Internet will eventually be captured and harnessed by the experienced political actors, and as a result, any change will be marginal, preventing a shift in the basic power balance of the political systems in democratic nations. In this view the use of the Internet will be "normalized" into the current electoral paradigm (Bimber and Davis 2003; Ward, Gibson, and Lusolli 2003; Margolis and Resnick 2000). In application, the supporters of normalization see the Internet as a new tool to be used as part of the conventional campaign structure. The structure would remain largely unmoved. In the United States, electoral politics has developed a two-party system that relies on a well-established structure of fundraising, constituent service, and mass media saturation to obtain results (Fiorina 1989). Depending on which scholarship one adopts, the Internet will either balance out the structural limitations of the system or become just another part of it.

In this book, we reject both approaches. While we have no desire to minimize the impact and importance of the previous scholarship, we suggest there is a larger narrative to tell. Both academic camps are attempting to fit the Internet into the traditional electoral system and predict or measure how its use can alter the dynamics and shift outcomes. We suggest this approach is self-limiting. The Internet does not fit into this system; it will make the traditional paradigm obsolete. At the most basic level, we are examining a change in the way people talk to each other, gather information, and learn. This might seem a small thing when compared with continent-shaking wars, consciousness-shifting ideas or philosophies, or even the millions or billions of dollars that the entertainment industry claims that Internet file-sharing has cost them. None of the above are small things. We do not dismiss them. In truth, they are all symptoms of the transformation we study in this book. The

Internet has changed the very nature of how people and society engage with one another. It is a medium that makes everyone your neighbor. It makes the vastness of human knowledge available in homes around the globe. It makes interactive communication possible at an increasingly low cost. It makes the transmission of ideas, images, and humanity itself available in ways unimaginable just a few short years ago. It is not altering the rules; it is changing the electoral game itself and creating a new paradigm.

Perhaps calling this change "revolutionary" smacks of hyperbole. There is nothing particularly new about the notion that states and societies evolve and change. There have been many technological improvements during the relatively short history of the American state. Literacy and newspapers helped bring about mass suffrage. The radio changed campaigning and governing. Franklin D. Roosevelt's novel and significant use of radio broadcasts is studied today and the impact of those broadcasts on America was significant. At its inception, television was lauded and criticized for its influences on society as well. Further, it is indisputable that as a medium television has made significant shifts in society, especially in politics, where media consultants and even candidate grooming are now important parts of the campaign (Graber 2007). Television has even changed the balance of the branches of the American government. Presidential power has grown through the ability of presidents to reach out through television to speak directly to the American people in ways that our founding fathers would neither have conceived nor likely would have approved (Kernell 2006).

All of the technological changes in how we communicate with each other are important milestones. Each change influenced how we choose our leaders and even why we choose our leaders. It is a widely held belief that the visual medium of television has led to an electoral advantage for taller candidates (Sommers 2002). Nonetheless, we suggest that the Internet, while a progression on this continuum, is not another step, but rather a leap into a fundamentally different environment than has ever existed. Each advance prior to the Internet was a form of one-way mass communication. In the simplest sense, news has historically been a singular message from a small group distributed to the larger society as a whole. Though they were not entirely one way (newspapers did have pages for readers' letters), the direction of the transmission was overwhelmingly unidirectional. Leaders or media spoke, and the people were the audience.

The mainstream media, such as newspapers and broadcasts, were ways for those with means to transmit ideas and information to the mass public. While surely significant in the operation of a society and a democracy, the conversation largely had one party talking and another party listening. Corporations, governments, or other groups of influence controlled the information conveyed with laws or sometimes simply by owning the means of distribution (Bennett 2008). In addition, the information itself is limited in time, scope, and content. A newspaper has a finite amount of space and it cannot be updated after it is printed. The content is limited to what was known at the time of printing and the number of pages available. Even broadcasts, which are not frozen in time, are limited by the nature of the medium to address only one idea or event at a time. If the broadcast is not covering the issue important to the viewer, the viewer has no recourse, and cannot alter the nature of the program. The Internet has none of these limitations. It is the most versatile, comprehensive interactive form of communication that exists or has ever existed, and it grows more interactive and accessible with each day that passes.

At its most basic, the Internet captures all of the elements of the previous mediums. In operation, the Internet can convey everything that television, magazines, radio, and newspapers do, and in a more timely manner with an easily accessible interface. The Internet can convey every type of visual and audio information on demand. Yet, beyond being simply a compilation of the previous mass media, the Internet presents the first two-way mass conversation. One can respond to a video with a video. One can discover an issue, research that issue and respond to it, and then respond to the responses or even chat about it, and distribute it to networks of other people from any of a multitude of mobile or fixed computing devices. Content can be organized, understood, and engaged using multiple applications, restricted only by the access and knowledge of the user.

Further, the Internet has no single gatekeeper. Anyone can create a website given sufficient knowledge and resources. While this is a limitation of sorts, it is a very low threshold established by the virtually uncountable proliferation of webpages. Search engines catalogue information so efficiently that any person with Internet access can find information on virtually any topic they can type into a search query. Even when drawn to Internet websites of the traditional media, users can easily move to secondary or alternative websites if desired. Evolving webpages, sometimes called Web 2.0, even allow users to personalize news or entertainment webpages by indicating what they want to see, hear, or read. The Internet has made information, and the gathering of it, virtually free for millions of people. Further, it connects people to each other and binds them with no concern for distance, geography, or traditional political cleavages. Unlike other media, the communications can be immediate. The feedback is immediate and the discovery of some information and its distribution is at speeds never before seen. The growth of broadband connections has multiplied the speed and newer technology will likely make the distribution limitless in breadth and scope. As the Internet grows and its penetration throughout the world increases, the changes will accelerate. The nature of the way society is linked with itself and with the state is shifting around us.

Since ideas are the engine of change, altering the very nature and speed of the transition of ideas quickly becomes paradigm changing. The movement of ideas cannot happen when there is little or no means to transmit the ideas. While one may build a better mousetrap, no one will appear at the door unless word of the invention makes its way beyond the entrance itself. In the context of institutional adaptation, the transmission of ideas within the greater society and between that society and its institutions is dependent on communication technology. The absence of such technology is limiting. In a nation of as vast a size as the United States, one may believe in the value of direct democracy, but such a belief is largely irrelevant in the absence of any ability to translate each person's opinions and decisions directly because of limited technologies. Representative democracy is not only justifiable through the concept of trusteeship, it has been the only possible and functional type of democracy because of the restrictions of poor communication over sizable distances. In the infancy of the United States, it simply was not possible to consult the people daily, weekly, or even annually for policy decisions. Nonetheless, by the twentieth century, technology had improved to such an extent that contemporaries of the period were openly discussing and publishing ideas about the use of direct democracy. The referendum and the initiative were readily discussed because of the new technology which improved communication and transportation. As noted in a published debate in 1912, voting technology for use in a referendum or initiative had improved to such a degree that the states could now proceed from the point where they were previously forced to stop (Beatson 1912).

Retrospective evaluation of the impact of technology is an easier task than the one we attempt here. Ascertaining change as an ongoing concern is far more difficult. Part of the measurement challenge is that the rapidity of the shifts makes static measures inefficient. That is to say what is true about how people use the Internet in 2010 might bear very little resemblance to the Internet use and penetration four or even two years later. Even the means by which people access the Internet is constantly changing. We have gone from desktops, to mobile computing, to telephones that are essentially small specialized computers. Multiple applications across various technology platforms are invented and adopted at unprecedented rates. This has led to changes in habits and behavior that are not confined to personal behavior. Members of Congress are now sending short messages to "followers" during political events using the communications protocol called Twitter (Newton-Small 2009). Twitter allows politicians to communicate with constituents and supporters in brief messages that can be transmitted from almost anywhere at any time, including the gallery during the president's State of the Union address. Political events can be organized immediately or even accidentally through a continual bombardment of information. Information, and perhaps even misinformation, is added to the discourse with a striking pace. No one knows what innovation in the next few years will mean or even what the innovation will be. As speeds increase across the network, the different ways people interact with each other will only be limited by ingenuity and imagination. By the time you read this book, it is possible that Twitter has evolved into something else or has been replaced by an even more creative communication protocol. It is even likely that as time passes you will be accessing this book through some type of easily distributed digital protocol rather than on any tangible physical medium like paper.

Yet even with these limitations, we can create a theoretical framework to understand these changes. Initially, we must establish how change in an otherwise stable democracy occurs. For our purposes, we want to step away from the overt forces of change brought about through the violent overthrow of a government or the explicit rejection and replacement of a government or governing system. While such times of change are clearly important, the focus on those moments can obscure the more regular shifts, adaptation, and evolution that happen as an ongoing concern in almost any state. The United States, like every nation, has had significant moments of societal evolution or even revolution. American democracy is constantly evolving and changing. Our history demonstrates that the nation is to be understood as a process, not as an end. As ascertained in his study of America, Alexis de Tocqueville noted, "[a] democracy can only obtain truth as the result of experience" (Tocqueville 2000: 181). To suggest experience matters is to suggest that society and the state can both learn and evolve. If experience matters, the workings of the government can be understood in less static positions. For any state that exists over significant periods, events often drive changes in how people interact with each other and with the state itself. Society and government engage in a constant interaction which forces adaptations and shifts in each other.

This is especially true in the United States despite the seemingly stable constitutional governing structure. Shifts in perception, operation, or even interpretation of the foundational documents can force fundamental changes in the overarching structure. Over time, the confluence of these sometimes subtle shifts changes the understanding of politics and the practice of politics in significant ways that were not initially foreseen. The changes may be so subtle and natural that they are largely unseen by contemporary participants. This process is driven by the interaction of the institutional structure of our government with stimuli it receives from the people. More directly, significant events and changes in our culture and society happen, and our government adapts to address them. This can occur in a number of ways, but most frequently it is largely the result of a change in the circumstance, belief, or even demographic makeup of the nation that is not anticipated by the structure or function of the state institutions.

To address these changes, which we will refer to as stimuli, the institutions adapt, but often in subtle and incremental ways. The source of the stimuli is often generated outside the institutional structure, as is the case when change is the result of an improvement in industrial or communications technology. However, stimuli can also be the product of the state institutions themselves as they interact and engage with elements of society, which in turn adapt to the institutions, and reflect their adaptations back in the manner and scope of their engagement with the institutions. Often this process occurs over larger temporal periods and a wider view is needed to see the effects of the social and institutional context in which government institutions must operate.

While the influence of the Internet as a stimulus for change remains our focus, it is worth noting at this point that other stimuli are regularly applied to the system, forcing changes. The Industrial Revolution not only changed the nature of American economics, but also increased the importance of trade and a federal government that regulates trade. This in turn changed the value of service in Congress, making it increasingly significant in developing professional legislators instead of the anticipated cadre of elite politicians (Dodd 1981). The use of party structure and the adoption of institutional rules to address these changes altered the nature of the governing process (Dodd 1981).

Society is constantly evolving, because people make choices. Agrarian economies may become industrial-shifting rural societies, and then urban ones. Social norms evolve, changing the family, group, and even individual dynamic. People themselves change and start to value things differently from previous generations. The state does not respond to such change by remaining static and fixed to either its historical roots or foundational structure. It changes and evolves. Sometimes the change is overt, as in a constitutional amendment or a new rules structure. Sometimes the change is subtle, as in placing a new or different meaning on what equal protection means. Like the society in which it exists, the state is constantly changing and evolving to address the pressures or stimuli applied to it in its dynamic relationship with the greater society.

The power of the Internet differs from most of the stimuli applied to the state. While states regularly adjust to changing beliefs in society, the Internet is not a belief. It is the means by which ideas are exchanged between people and with the various elements of the state. The Internet changes how beliefs are obtained and disseminated. It changes how conversations are held and who gets to speak. It changes the location of the public sphere and brings it into homes and offices. The essential element of understanding the evolution of power within American institutions is the interactive relationships of the people with each other and with the instruments of the state. The Internet penetrates through all institutions and its power to shape and reshape public opinion is unprecedented. Already the distinctions between private and public information are difficult to define. Jurgen Habermas noted that the boundaries between state and society have blurred, making formal distinctions between the two spheres difficult to delineate (Habermas 1991). The Internet presents a new kind of stimuli that changes the very nature of how this relationship exists. It is the transmission of information to anyone from anyone with almost no boundaries at all.

There is no doubt that the Internet is a potent force, but the question is one of magnitude. In this book, we will isolate effects of this technology and measure impacts. Technological changes can impact an array of human relationships with each other and with both public and private institutions. Technology itself can exist as an exogenous stimulus that affects society. It can change how people interact, how they work, or even how they vote. This substantive change in people or society can then affect how state institutions operate. If there is a change in communication, it might affect how people evaluate political information, or how they see and understand politicians or political candidates. This can alter how society engages with institutions. It may lead to the ascendance of a political group or demographic group that is well situated to adapt to and take advantage of the technological stimuli. If the control of a state institution changes, then public policy will change as well, with society then having to alter itself to adjust and react to the new policies. While it might at first seem that the impact of a new technology such as the Internet is largely an issue of efficiency, we will demonstrate that this significant technological advancement is forcing adaptation and evolution.

While ideas are potent engines of change, the means to effect change can be as important, and can even work in conjunction with new conceptual understandings of the state, as was the case with voting technology and the referendum. We seek to isolate technology as a variable, because it can have a significant effect in creating change even in the absence of a conceptual shift simply by maximizing the voices of those with access and knowledge over those without. The Internet changes the means and operation of the system at a fundamental level by adding a new procedural lens to the equation. While superficially this type of change can be seen as an ideological movement in the population, it really is nothing more than changing what we are counting and how we are counting it. By using a measure that favors one group or demographic over another, the result can be skewed to favor one outcome over another (Riker 1986).

If the change is of sufficient magnitude, the alteration alone is enough to redefine representation and politics themselves even when the rule system defining representation and the political system remain unchanged. Technology as a stimulus can change the entire interactive dynamic between the society and the government by affecting people's behavior, and as a result, affecting how and to what degree they engage with state institutions. If technology favors one group over another in political participation, then the end result will be a government which is more responsive to the advantaged groups, and policies will be implemented that are favorable to that group.

The implications of the Internet are wide and varied. Some are relatively easy to anticipate. As noted above, some better prepared groups are likely to be advantaged by their knowledge of the Internet. Political actors are likely to use the technology to enhance their image, raise funds, and rally supporters, though probably in conjunction with the more traditional elements of the mass media. States are using the technology to increase efficiencies in communications with citizens both for bureaucratic and political activities. Information that previously could be obtained only at government offices is now regularly posted on the Internet for review. Yet, these are the simplest of possibilities. As we will show in the chapters of this book, the long-term implications are much more far reaching.

In chapter 2, we set the predicate for our examination by presenting the foundation for the narrative told here. We begin with an analysis of the descriptive measures used in this book and explore some of the foundational questions that the Internet raises in the political context, beginning with an understanding of who uses the technology and for what purpose. We focus this analysis by examining data on social networking, political participation, and campaigning. This survey of the data sets a predicate to apply more advanced and focused methodologies in later chapters. Again, this is the primary contribution of this book; we seek to offer empirical evidence in support of many of the theories that have been offered in the literature but have not actually been tested.

In chapter 3, we expand our assessment of the Internet into a larger review of the impact of an interactive Internet society. We contend that there are lower costs associated with using the Internet to gather information than with traditional sources, and as a result, individuals who use the Internet have greater opportunities to develop knowledge about politics. Further, we argue that the disparity between the "haves" and "have-nots" when it comes to use of the Internet, or the *digital divide*, may exacerbate the knowledge gap that already exists. We claim that this is revolutionizing American politics, as the knowledge of one's government is important, if not essential, to effective participation in democracy.

In chapter 4 we move to empirical tests of the possible changes as a result of the integration of the Internet into the political machinery and environment. We test the impact of Internet voting by creating a theoretical framework for understanding the effect of Internet voting on the electorate. Based on standard Downsian rational choice voting theory, we claim that Internet voting lowers the cost of voting for certain voting demographics based upon race, age, and income. We further contend that this electoral advantage may crystallize the growing turnout disparity between demographic groups. Using data from Internet voting we assess this theory.

In chapter 5, we move beyond electoral mechanisms and explore the impact of the Internet on the dominant theories of political participation and the largely pessimistic assessment of participation in general. We present an alternative view of the American political future that is substantively different from the theories of declining participation and lower rates of belief in the system that have dominated the scholarship on political behavior. In addition, we accept the underlying understanding that democracy is rooted in an understanding of social networks and communicated ideas, but propose with empirical data that the Internet is a solution to decaying social capital and the decline of political participation. We review the evidence to show that the Internet promotes social capital through networking with a speed and interactivity that was never before possible. While the ultimate implications of this modern Internet society are unclear and will be for some time, the initial data suggest that there is a far more rich and diverse engagement of people with government than political scientists have been willing to concede.

In chapters 6 and 7 we move to a focused assessment of the Internet in society. In chapter 6, we review the implications of the Internet on the increasingly polarized American electorate. Combining data on Internet usage and public opinion we illustrate how the nature and utilization of the Internet may be contributing to a more polarized America. Continuing our focus on societal effects, we explore the nature of campaign funding in the Internet age and how the Internet is democratizing the participation of citizens in the campaign through open and effective outreach. We expand this assessment of the Internet campaign in chapter 8 where we explore just how effective webpages are in helping candidates compete in and win elections. Using data from the 2006 midterm elections, we explore how webpage success correlates with electoral success, and how webpages ultimately change how campaigns are won or lost in the new Internet age.

Finally, we conclude the analysis in chapter 9 by assessing the importance of the Internet as a general concern in light of all of our data. We present a larger theory tying each of our findings to illustrate the power of the Internet to change the very bedrock of the electoral system. We end our analysis with projections and predictions concerning what the future of American politics will be as the Internet continues to evolve and penetrate the electoral system and the greater society.

2

A Descriptive Summary of the Measurement and Story

As detailed in chapter 1, we argue in this book that the Internet is stimulating foundational changes in the operation of politics in the United States. Each chapter that follows empirically addresses a different topic using a combination of election and survey data. Considered together, we think the evidence provides substantial support to our overall contention that the Internet is shifting both the way politics happen and the end results. The following chapter lays out the foundation for our narrative by describing the measures used in this book. These descriptions put the findings in a context by answering some of the foundational questions: How prevalent is Internet use? How many people actually use the Internet to gather political information? Do people claim to learn from the Internet and what do they actually know about some of the basics of U.S. politics? Will people vote via the Internet if given the option? How much social networking is taking place on the Internet? How are people using the Internet to gather information? Finally, how pervasive is the web presence of political candidates? With these issues addressed, we will move to a more focused look at specific measures suggesting larger political implications.

In addition to the baseline data, the following chapter describes all of the data used in the book including the sources, sample sizes, and collection procedures. This description is followed by a discussion of all the primary variables used in each chapter.[1] This discussion includes the operationalization of all measures with tabular and graphical displays of their distributions.

In this discussion, we highlight the theory, findings, and relationship across the chapters. This description helps lay the foundation for the chapters that follow by providing a context from which to interpret the findings. We begin by describing the data.

DATA

There are many different ways to measure the Internet and its usage, beginning with surveys of individual preference and including fixed measures of actual Internet traffic. We rely on several data sources throughout this book. We use data from two different surveys, election data gathered on the 2000 Democratic primary in the state of Arizona, Internet search engine data, and national data gathered on the 2006 U.S. Congressional election. The four sources of survey data are the Pew Internet & American Life Project 2006 and 2008 Post-Election Tracking Surveys as well as the 2008 Civic Engagement Survey and a survey of college students from a variety of classes at the University of Louisville and Florida Atlantic University.[2] The data are widely drawn to present a reliable cross-section of America.

The 2006 and 2008 Post-Election Pew projects randomly surveyed, respectively, 2,562 and 2,254 U.S. residents immediately following the 2006 and 2008 November U.S. Congressional elections, and the Civic Engagement Survey polled 2,251 respondents in August 2008. All include both random-digit-dialed and cell phone respondents. Respondents were at least eighteen years of age. The datasets contain questions about the elections and sources of information about the campaign including several batteries of questions about Internet use for gathering and disseminating political information. The Internet and its influence on politics are constantly changing. This is why we used multiple national datasets. This allows us to look at the changes over a two-year period, and also allows us to draw comparisons to our Student Data. The survey of college students with similar questions was conducted in February and March 2008. The sample of 666 respondents (70 percent from the University of Louisville and 30 percent from Florida Atlantic University) consists of students from a variety of political science and business courses, both lower and upper division. There are a total of eighteen different courses with six sections of a lower division American federal government class containing students from a multitude of majors. Instructors for each course were given instructions on how to administer the survey. They were not allowed to answer questions that involved explaining the items. Respondents anonymously filled out a paper form that included the questions and response categories.

The student sample is obviously not a national sample, as are the Pew Data, yet these data present an interesting case study of student populations. As we will address in more detail in later chapters, the generational variation in Internet use is significant and the student usage allows for a likely preview of future usage as the younger generation begins to replace the older ones. These data can give us some sense of what to expect when it comes to Internet use and political behavior in the future. There is significant overlap in the indicators in each dataset, so we compare results wherever possible.

While survey data do present a window on usage, we also rely on election data as more concrete measures of actual behavior. The first set of election data we use is from the 2000 Democratic primary in the state of Arizona. The data are a compilation of turnout results from the 2000 Arizona Democratic Presidential Preference Primary and demographic data obtained from the Bureau of the U.S. Census. The turnout results were obtained from the Arizona Democratic Party and were available at the party's official website. These data are formatted as whole numbers representing turnout by county across several categories including total turnout, remote Internet turnout, mail-in turnout, polling place Internet turnout, and polling place paper turnout. The data provide for fifteen cases based on the number of counties in Arizona. The demographic data are also grouped by county and coded as whole numbers, which enables the compilation of each of these sources. These data are aggregate. This small sample size is addressed by using a Bayesian approach that will be further explained in chapter 4.

In addition, we use election data from the 2006 U.S. Congressional midterm election gathered from a variety of sources. They are a compilation of turnout results, web presence and web traffic indicators, and a host of controls from eighty-six separate races in the 2006 election (106 House candidates and 67 Senate candidates, N = 173). We selected the races that were deemed competitive by Congressional Quarterly, Inc., and included the two leading candidates (incumbent and challenger or the two leading vote-getters for open seats).[3] The webpage ranking data come from Google, Inc., an Internet search engine company that also offers other services including PageRank, which estimates web presence. We also use data from Alexa, a web information company. The elections data come from the Federal Election Committee and can be obtained at http://www.TheGreenPapers.com. We also use U.S. Census data to measure education by state. Finally, data used for political experience control variables were obtained at http://wikipedia.org.[4]

HOW PERVASIVE IS INTERNET USE?

Even without the more complex data analysis which we will do in following chapters, our Internet data begin to describe a new type of political environment in America. The impact the Internet is having and will have on politics is dependent on how pervasive Internet use is and will become. The data illustrate that there is a growing trend toward using the Internet as a source for communication and information across fields of knowledge, but clearly involving political knowledge. Nonetheless, while the Internet may change how people behave and engage in politics, that change is only relevant if the Internet has enough usage and penetration in society to matter. We can begin to construct a picture of the Internet and its usage among the public with our data. This will provide a foundation for our later findings within an empirical context. The Pew Data have indicators that give us a broad estimate by measuring the volume of Internet use and access from work and home.[5]

Initially, it is apparent from the surveys that the use of the Internet is increasing rapidly. The data reflect that Internet use was substantial in 2006 (figure 2.1). Over 65 percent of those surveyed claimed to use the Internet at least occasionally. The growth of the Internet and its penetration into the general public has been trending upward with significant growth over a short period, which is expected to continue (Jones and Fox 2009). This is also reflected in figure 2.1. The percent who claimed to use the Internet has increased significantly to near 70 percent in the 2008 data. For our purposes, the basic predicate is set. The numbers are large enough for the Internet to have a significant impact if use is indeed consequential. In fact, the rise in usage over the past decade is so significant and is moving with such rapidity, even in the absence of universal Internet adoption by the public, that projections of changes based on expected Internet growth are reasonable and appropriate.

Figure 2.1 details the number of people using the Internet, but it does not reveal the frequency of use. The results presented in table 2.1 address this concern by focusing on how often people who responded affirmatively to the previous question use the Internet. People who use the Internet are slightly more likely to use it at work. Many people do not have access to the Internet from

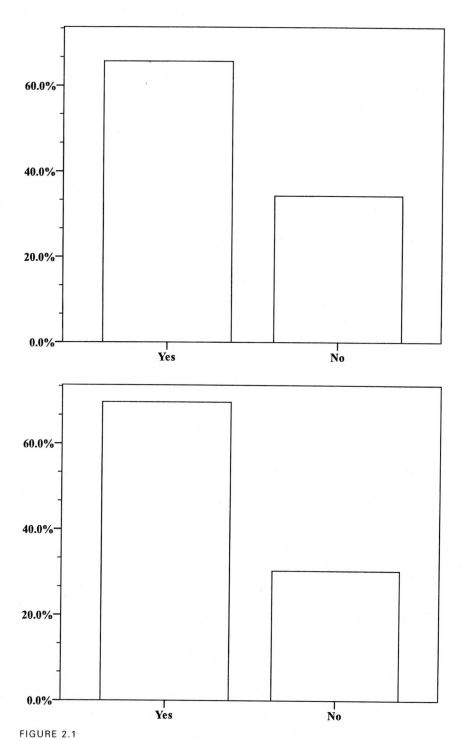

FIGURE 2.1

Do People Use the Internet at Least Occasionally?

Sources: (top) 2006 Pew post-election data; (bottom) 2008 Pew post-election data.

Table 2.1.   Frequency People Use the Internet at Home and Work

	Home		Workplace	
	2006	*2008*	*2006*	*2008*
Never	90 (5.3)	104 (6.6)	654 (38.9)	728 (46.0)
Less Often	69 (4.1)	72 (4.5)	62 (3.7)	33 (2.1)
Every Few Weeks	74 (4.4)	67 (4.2)	28 (1.7)	19 (1.2)
1–2 Days a Week	190 (11.3)	200 (12.6)	229 (13.6)	64 (4.0)
3–5 Days a Week	404 (24.0)	258 (16.3)	82 (4.9)	64 (4.0)
About Once a Day	378 (22.5)	371 (23.4)	136 (8.1)	114 (7.2)
Several Times a Day	478 (28.4)	513 (32.4)	492 (29.2)	560 (35.4)
Number of Cases	1683	1585	1683	1582

Note: Data come from the Pew Internet & American Life Project, November 2006 and 2008 Post-Election Tracking Surveys. Percentage in parentheses.

work. Nevertheless, the numbers for both home and work suggest people are using the Internet quite frequently. One of the central premises of this book is that the impact of the Internet on politics is likely to increase in the coming years. The increasing frequency of use of the Internet could contribute to this effect. This increase is evidenced in the change from 2006 to 2008. In 2006, 28.4 percent claimed to use the Internet several times a day from home and in 2008 32.4 percent made this claim. 29.2 percent claimed to use the Internet several times a day from work in 2006, and in 2008 this rose to 35.4 percent. Altogether, these numbers suggest that Internet use is fairly common.

A parallel measure is included in the student survey as well as a question about the frequency of Internet use.[6] As expected, student Internet use is much higher than the general population. As can be seen in figure 2.2, around 66 percent claim to go online more than once a day. The percentage continues to get smaller as each response option decreases. In fact, not one student in the sample claimed to "never go online." This is the first indicator of an assertion we will make in greater detail in later chapters that the impact of the Internet is only likely to increase as older generations are replaced with younger ones. The Student Data are comprised of those who are likely participants in the process as they age. The combination of the frequency of usage in both datasets certainly suggests that low usage of the Internet will not prevent it from having a great impact on politics. For this to happen, though, people must be using the Internet for political purposes. The next section addresses this very question.

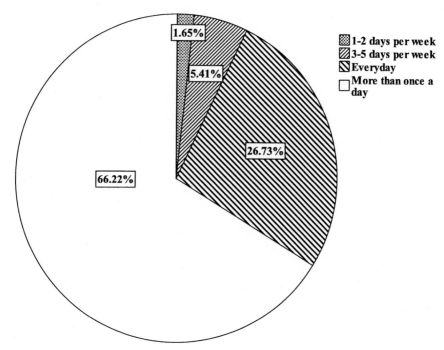

1-2 days per week
3-5 days per week
Everyday
More than once a day

1.65%

5.41%

26.73%

66.22%

FIGURE 2.2
Frequency Students Go Online
Source: 2008 student data.

POLITICAL KNOWLEDGE AND THE INTERNET

In chapter 3, we will explore in detail the influence that media/information consumption by means of the Internet has on individual levels of political knowledge. An initial review of the data illustrates that there is a positive influence. Increased consumption is associated with higher levels of knowledge. The costs for individuals of gathering and learning from information on the Internet are critical in assessing its impact. Yet, to reach this issue, we must focus on the preliminary question of whether people are relying on the Internet as a source of news. In the Pew Data, the following indicator is used to measure people's primary source of news: "How have you been getting most of your news about the November elections?" Possible answers are "from television, from newspapers, from radio, from magazines, or from the Internet." In the Student Data, a similar indicator is used: "How have you been getting most of your news about the presidential election campaign?" The answer choices are the same: "from television, from newspapers, from radio, from magazines, or from the Internet."[7]

The results in table 2.2 suggest that while the Internet is increasing in popularity, it has yet to become the dominant source of news and information. This is not surprising considering that the development and widespread accessibility of the Internet, especially broadband technology, is still in its infancy. Nonetheless, some interesting conclusions can be drawn by looking at the distributions for each dataset and by comparing results across datasets. The results suggest, not surprisingly, that television is still the most used source of news. In the Pew Data, 61 percent of those surveyed in 2006 and 69 percent in 2008 claimed that television was their primary source, compared to nearly 53 percent in the Student Data. Roughly 21 percent relied on newspapers in the 2006 Pew Data and around 11 percent in 2008, relative to only 9 percent of the students surveyed. In the 2006 Pew Data, 10 percent relied on the radio and for 2008 it was nearly 7 percent, compared to nearly 8 percent of the students. Finally, less than 1 percent primarily used magazines in the 2006 and 2008 Pew Data and just over 2 percent in the Student Data.

Further, and perhaps most interesting, is the comparisons of those who rely primarily on the Internet for news across the data. First, the comparison of the 2006 to the 2008 Pew Data suggests that the use of the Internet for news is growing. Roughly 8 percent of those in the 2006 Pew Data claimed to use the Internet as their primary source of news, while nearly 11 percent in 2008 data made this claim. This is a substantial increase in just two years. That said,

Table 2.2. How People Have Been Getting News about Elections

	Pew Data				Student Data	
	2006		2008		2008	
	Count	%	Count	%	Count	%
Television	1564	61.0	1556	69.0	351	52.7
Newspapers	529	20.6	254	11.3	60	9.0
Radio	256	10.0	156	6.9	52	7.8
Magazines	19	0.7	16	.7	15	2.3
Internet	194	7.6	245	10.9	153	23.0
Other	—	—	27	1.2	35	5.3
Number of Cases	2562	100%	2254	100%	666	100%

Note: Data come from the Pew Internet & American Life Project, November 2006 and 2008 Post-Election Tracking Surveys, and a 2008 survey of college students at the University of Louisville and Florida Atlantic University. The "other" response was volunteered in the 2008 Pew Data.

23 percent of the students surveyed claimed that the Internet is their primary source of news. This is a non-trivial number of people in all three datasets, but the high number in the Student Data suggests a long-term generational trend. As we will review in later chapters, initial measures of the usage of the Internet suggest a digital divide in which the young and the educated are most likely to rely on the Internet for information. Since the Student Data are dominated by both youth and education, the high number should be expected. The figure 23 percent illustrates a movement away from physical newspapers, which remain the second most used information source in the broader-based Pew Data. Newspapers are a rapidly declining resource in the Student Data. Putting aside the educational and age-based trends, Internet growth as a source for knowledge is rising across almost all demographics. The numbers in both datasets are significantly higher than ten years ago. If usage continues to grow at this rate, the Internet will at some point become the primary news outlet for most regardless of age or education.

The available data allow us to focus this question beyond whether people use the Internet to gather information and look more closely at how the Internet is used for political knowledge and interaction. There are multiple indicators of how people engage with the electoral and political environment in these datasets.[8] The Pew Data contain indicators representing the types of information sought and reviewed as well as the types of engagement the voters might have online with campaigns and other voters. Similar indicators were placed in the Student Data and the measures present an interesting window into online political participation.

Some of the results presented in table 2.3 are based on those surveyed in the Pew Data who responded affirmatively to the question, "Do you use the Internet, at least occasionally?" There were 1,683 out of the total 2,562 who responded affirmatively (65.7 percent) in the 2006 data and 1,568 out of 2,254 (69.6 percent) in the 2008 data. The other results for 2006 are based on those who responded affirmatively to the question, "Did you get any news or information about the November elections on the Internet or through e-mail?" There were 657 who responded affirmatively. The filter question in 2008 was, "Did you ever go online to get news or information about the 2008 elections?" There were 918 who responded affirmatively (58.5 percent).

While the numbers are still not majorities across many of the items, there are large groups of people who claimed they used the Internet for a range of different political purposes and the trend is clearly toward the Internet, but it is important to remember that under 70 percent claimed to use the Internet at all; a minority of those claimed to get information about the election in 2006, while there was a majority in 2008. Thus, the results that follow must be considered in this context. Respectively, 39 and nearly 59 percent of the respondents in 2006 and 2008 claimed they obtained news about the upcoming elections on the Internet. Both are sizable percentages, though the most striking aspect is the 20 percent increase from 2006 to 2008, when a substantial majority of Internet users used online resources to learn about the elections. Roughly 17 percent of respondents said they sent or received e-mails about the campaigns in 2006, and nearly 48 percent in 2008. Over 32 percent stated that they had come across campaign information on the Internet in 2006. Approximately 68 percent claimed to have obtained information about the 2006 U.S. Senate race; this figure dropped to nearly 50 percent in 2008. Also, around 64 percent claimed to see something about the 2006 U.S. House race, though this dropped to 37 percent in 2008, roughly 64 percent about the 2006 gubernatorial race in their state, and near 25 percent in 2008, and about 51 percent said they viewed information about 2006 local races compared to almost 44 percent in 2008. Perhaps these lower numbers in 2008 are a result of heightened attention to the presidential race. In addition, approximately 49 percent claimed to view information about ballot measures in 2006, dropping to approximately 39 percent in 2008. Unsurprisingly, the highest percentage response in 2008 was concerning the presidential race. In 2008, around 79 percent claimed to have obtained information online about the campaign for president.

There are also large groups who claimed they looked on the Internet for more information about candidates' positions (around 57 percent in 2006 and 68 percent in 2008), looked for endorsements (approximately 26 percent in 2006), checked the accuracy of candidates' claims (roughly 39 percent in 2006), and viewed videos (about 34 percent in 2006 and around 68 percent in 2008). Additionally, about 9 percent signed up to be placed on e-mail lists in 2006 and nearly 17 percent in 2008. The data also contained items measuring if respondents had gathered information via portal news sites like Yahoo.com (approximately 61 percent in 2006 and 58 percent in 2008), network news websites (around 64 percent in 2006 and 69 percent in 2008), major newspaper websites (roughly 35 percent in 2006 and 38 percent in 2008), and local news organization websites (approximately 51 percent in 2006 and 2008). Taken together, the results contained in table 2.3 suggest that many are using the Internet to gather political information in a variety of ways.

As for the Student Data, the distributions of activities on the Internet to gather political information displayed in table 2.3 suggest that the young are also relying on the Internet for information quite extensively. Nearly 37

Table 2.3. Political Information Gathering on the Internet

	% Did this	
Pew Data	2006	2008
Get News about Election	39.0	58.5
Send or Receive E-mails about Campaign	16.9	47.5
Come across Campaign News	32.6	—
Number of Cases	1683	1568
See Anything about U.S. Senate Race	68.2	49.7
See Anything about U.S. House Race	64.4	37.1
See Anything about Governor's Race	64.2	25.1
See Anything about Local Races	57.3	43.9
See Anything about Ballot Measures	48.6	39.4
See Anything about the Race for President	—	79.4
Look at Candidates' Positions/Records	56.9	67.6
Look for Candidates' Endorsements	25.7	—
Check the Accuracy of Claims	39.4	—
View Video Clips about Candidates	33.8	56.8
Sign up to Receive Campaign E-mail/Updates	8.7	16.7
Look at Portal News	60.6	57.8
Look at Network T.V. News	64.4	69.2
Look at Major Newspapers	35.0	38.3
Look at Local News Organizations	50.8	51.3
Number of Cases	657	918
Student Data		
Send or Receive E-mails about Campaign		36.9
Join Online Discussions about Election		10.4
Find out about Campaign Organizations		27.6
Read Opinions on Networking Sites		42.5
View Political Videos		54.1
Number of Cases		666

Note: Data come from the Pew Internet & American Life Project, November 2006 and 2008 Post-Election Tracking Surveys, and a 2008 survey of college students at the University of Louisville and Florida Atlantic University.

percent claimed to have sent or received e-mails about a campaign, just over 10 percent have had online discussions about the upcoming election, approaching 28 percent have gone on the Internet to find out about campaign organizations, and over 42 percent claimed to have read opinions on networking sites. Interestingly, a majority of respondents claimed to have viewed political videos. This is the only majority claim in either dataset. Finally, because the frequency that college students go online to get news about the election was an ordinal variable, we decided to present it graphically as opposed to the tabular form we used for the other dichotomous variables. The findings presented in figure 2.3 here suggest that most do go online for news about elections at least sometimes. In fact, a majority claimed to go online for election news at least one to two days per week (51.7 percent), 30. 2 percent less than 1 to 2 days per week, and only 18.2 percent claimed to never go online to obtain news about the election.

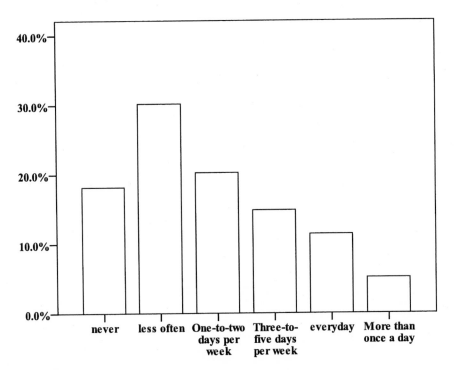

FIGURE 2.3
Frequency Students Go Online to Get News about Elections

Source: 2008 student data.

The above presented distribution of Internet use and political information gathering provides a foundation for understanding the potential impact of the Internet on learning. People are using the Internet to gather information in increasing numbers with a clear upward trend, though whether this is resulting in actual learning is unclear. Before getting to our objective measure of knowledge, the Student Data had a series of questions designed to ascertain the respondents' subjective assessment of how much they learn from the Internet: "How often, if ever, do you learn something about the presidential campaign or the candidates from . . . (the websites of newspapers, other kinds of online news magazine and opinion sites such as Slate.com or the National Review online, personal blogs you read, candidate's personal websites)?" Each item was asked separately and respondents were given the following response options: "regularly, sometimes, hardly ever, or never" (range = 1–4).[9] The mean score for each of these items is presented in figure 2.4. Clearly, students

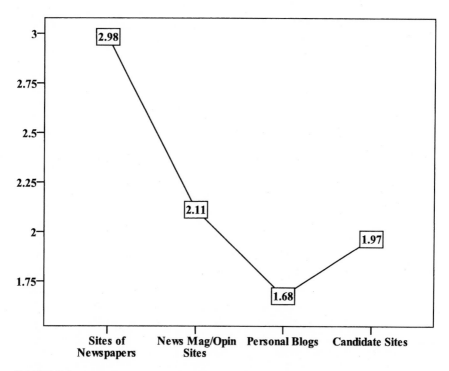

FIGURE 2.4
Mean Score for Students Who Claim to Learn from Websites
Source: 2008 student data.

claimed to learn the most from the websites of newspapers (mean = 2.98). This suggests that newspapers may have a more promising future online. Following newspapers are online news magazine and opinion sites with a mean score of 2.11. This is higher than the midpoint, but significantly lower than newspapers. The lowest of the four items used here is personal blogs (mean = 1.68). Candidates' websites are slightly higher at 1.98. Taken together, these numbers suggest that students believe they are learning from the Internet. Of course, these numbers are subjective assessments and may also simply reflect students' use of these sites. Regardless, the numbers indicate that they are using the Internet to gather information about politics.

Our central purpose in chapter 3 is to measure whether people actually learn about politics from the Internet. In this effort, we test to see if the above described indicators of information gathering and the claim to learn from the Internet do predict knowledge, *ceteris paribus.* While we will analyze this issue more closely in chapter 3, the initial findings do suggest that information gathering does stimulate knowledge. Our measure of *political knowledge* is based on three items from the Student Data. They are as follows:

- Do you know the name of the U.S. secretary of state?[10]
- Who has the final responsibility to decide if a law is constitutional or not—is it the president, Congress, or the Supreme Court? (President, Congress, Supreme Court, or don't know.)
- Would you say that one of the parties is more conservative than the other at the national level? If yes: Which party is more conservative? (Republicans, Democrats, neither/both the same, or don't know.)

For the first, responses indicating Condoleezza Rice were coded as a 1 for correct.[11] The other two questions were coded as 1 for correct if the response was the Supreme Court and Republicans respectively.[12] There was quite a bit of variation across these items. As displayed in table 2.4 only 48 percent correctly identified the secretary of state, around 70 percent correctly answered the question of who decides if a law is constitutional, and nearly 78 percent correctly identified which party was more conservative. These numbers are quite staggering considering these are college students and around 23 percent of them were political science majors. Each question was designed to have a differing level of difficulty and the marginal distributions

Table 2.4.   Percent Correct on Knowledge Indicators

	Frequency	Percent Correct
Who is the secretary of state?	320	48.0
Who decides if a law is constitutional?	469	70.4
Which party is more conservative?	516	77.5
Number of Cases	666	

Note: Data come from a 2008 survey of college students at the University of Louisville and Florida Atlantic University.

are consistent with these levels. The variation aids in making it a more useful dependent variable.

VOTING ON THE INTERNET

Chapter 3 explores the impact of information gathering via the Internet on political knowledge, making the theoretical argument that the digital divide contributes to a disproportionate effect between the "haves" and "have-nots." Chapter 4 extends this argument, making the case that allowing binding elections to take place over the Internet may, in fact, exacerbate traditional cleavages in voter turnout that are based on the haves and the have-nots by lowering the cost of voting. To date, the 2000 Arizona Democratic Presidential Primary is the only national election in the United States that has allowed voting on the Internet. Aside from the digital divide concern, the most striking result in this election was the dramatic effect on overall turnout. Turnout increased by 723 percent from 1996 to 2000 (Solop 2001). While the context of the election could have certainly played a role in this increase, the introduction of e-voting is hard to dismiss. The results presented in figure 2.5 make this point clear. Voters were given the option to vote in a traditional polling place, by mail, or on the Internet. We constructed a measure of Internet turnout by calculating the percentage of the total turnout by county (Internet turnout by county/total turnout by county). Across the fifteen counties in Arizona, the lowest total turnout by Internet relative to the other methods was just under 30 percent and the highest reached 50 percent. Large numbers of voters took advantage of the opportunity to vote using the Internet. In chapter 4, we will look more closely at these data and provide a theoretical foundation to explain the effects of the Internet as well as show directly the impact of Internet voting on the electorate.

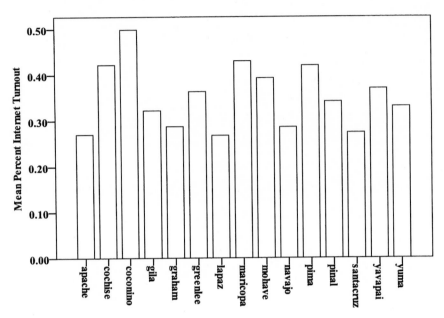

FIGURE 2.5
Distribution of E-voting across Fifteen Counties in Arizona
Source: 2000 Arizona Democratic presidential primary data.

RECONSIDERING INTERNET INFLUENCE ON PARTICIPATION

While chapter 4 directly looks at how the Internet could influence turnout if e-voting were allowed, chapter 5 suggests that the influence on turnout can also be less direct. To address this, we build on the widely held theory that suggests social networking contributes to stronger democratic society, or social capital, which stimulates political participation (Putnam 1995a, 1995b, 2000). We contend that the Internet is reinvigorating social capital by reconnecting people in a nontraditional manner. Specifically, we argue that social networking through networking sites and other Web 2.0 applications may actually encourage people to contribute to the political process by voting and/ or being civically engaged (writing letters, attending protests, attending political meetings, etc.). Both the Pew Civic Engagement data and Student Data contain a series of indicators of social networking via the Internet.[13]

The results presented in table 2.5 provide the marginal distributions on all of the networking indicators from the Pew Data and for the two items in the Student Data. The differences across the datasets here are quite revealing.

Table 2.5.   Social Networking on the Internet

	% Did not do this	% Did this
2008 Pew Civic Engagement Data		
Use a Social Networking Site	75.4	24.6
Create your own Journal or Blog	92.2	7.8
Use Twitter	96.2	3.8
Communicate w/Group using E-mail	88.0	12.0
Communicate w/Group using Website	95.6	4.4
Communicate w/Group using Networking Site	71.2	28.8
Number of Cases	2251	
Student Data		
Use a Social Networking Site	12.0	88.0
Use Social Networking to Learn about Campaign	49.8	50.2
Number of Cases	666	

Note: Data come from the Pew Internet & American Life Project, August 2008 Civic Engagement Survey, and a 2008 survey of college students at the University of Louisville and Florida Atlantic University. The first three Pew items were collapsed here (yes and yes, yesterday = did this). The first student item asked frequency and then was collapsed (never = did not do this). The second asked how important these sites were to learn about campaigns and this was also collapsed (not important = did not do this).

As expected, networking via the Internet is more prevalent in the Student Data. The student sample represents a younger population overall which is consistent with our previous measures. Social networking on the Internet finds greater usage among younger student groups. These results may be a glimpse of the increased magnitude of social networking via the Internet that we should expect as this generation ages and older generations are replaced.

Nonetheless, social networking via the Internet is not completely absent among the national sample. Nearly 25 percent of those in the Pew Data claimed to use social networking sites such as Facebook, MySpace, or LinkedIn. That said, this number reached 88 percent among students and over 50 percent claimed to learn about the campaign from social networking sites. The Pew Data also contain a series of other Web 2.0/social networking use indicators. Nearly 8 percent indicated that they have created an online journal or blog and almost 4 percent used Twitter (we expect this latter number has significantly gone up since 2008). Finally, the Pew Data include indicators of how people communicate with groups of which they are a member: 12 percent claimed to do so using e-mail, around 4 percent do so through the group's website, and nearly 29 percent use the group's social networking site. So, those represented in both samples are clearly using social networking sites and also beginning to use other Web 2.0 applications to connect to the political world.

MORE PARTICIPATION AND INFORMATION CONSUMPTION

We extend the participation model in chapter 6. In addition to social networking contributing to participation, we theorize that the Internet, as the new media, is disrupting traditional two-sided (impartial) information flows (Zaller 1992) and replacing them with two one-sided (partial) information flows resulting in a polarization effect on public opinion. In addition, we test whether this effect can actually stimulate political participation in the form of voting. In chapter 6, we will test this theory by modeling the effect of the Internet on dissemination of political information. Presently, and as a precursor to those models, we explore how often people prefer two-sided or one-sided information and the frequency with which people consume information from one-sided websites.

Respondents in the 2006 and 2008 Pew Post-Election Data who answered affirmatively to a question about whether they used the Internet to get any news about the election were asked the following question: "When you get political or campaign information online, would you say most of the sites you go to share your point of view, don't have a particular point of view, or challenge your own point of view?"[14] The distribution of responses is presented in figure 2.6. Near 30 percent of those sampled in both datasets claimed they preferred news that shared their point of view, while only around 20 percent claimed they preferred news that challenged their point of view in the 2006 data, and this estimate drops to about 16 percent in 2008. The majority claimed to prefer news that does not have a point of view (around 51 percent in 2006 and 53 percent in 2008), but we have reason to believe that this number may be over-estimated as a result of a social desirability effect (See Bardes and Oldendick 2007). The politically correct/socially desirable answer is to say that you prefer non-biased news. Likewise, people may also think another socially desirable response is to say that they prefer news that challenges their point of view. The claim to prefer news that shares one's point of view is not the socially desirable response. As a result, the data may well underestimate the percentage of those who actually consume one-sided information. Nevertheless, even if the data were perfectly accurate, 30 percent represents a significant block of the potential electorate.

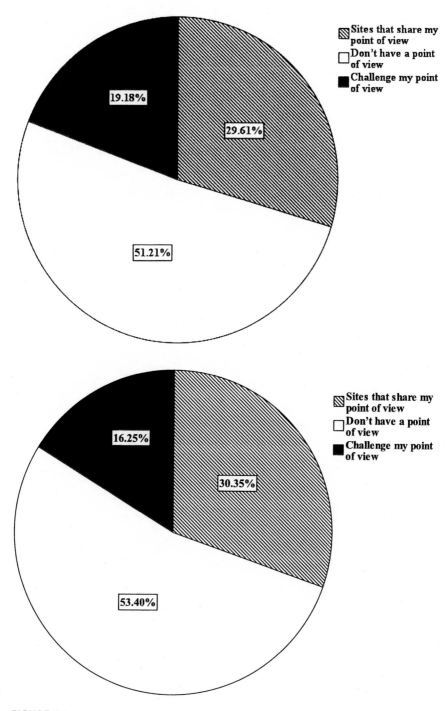

Sites that share my point of view

Don't have a point of view

Challenge my point of view

19.18%

29.61%

51.21%

Sites that share my point of view

Don't have a point of view

Challenge my point of view

16.25%

30.35%

53.40%

FIGURE 2.6

Preference for Bias in Online News

Sources: (top) 2006 Pew post-election data; (bottom) 2008 Pew post-election data.

The preference for one-sided information is pertinent to the theory we propose in chapter 6 but even more central is the actual consumption of one-sided information. Using the Pew Data, we were able to measure the usage of websites that we conceptualized as one-sided. These included: candidate websites, issue-oriented websites, online journals or blogs, and websites of ideological news organizations.[15] Among those who use the Internet to gather political information, nearly 21 percent visited candidates' sites in 2006, roughly 33 percent visited Barack Obama's site in 2008, and about 24 percent visited John McCain's site in 2008 (see table 2.6). Across usage of other types of one-sided sites, roughly 30 percent visited issue-oriented sites in 2006 and about 23 percent in 2008; about 22 and 23 percent in 2006 and 2008, respectively, read blogs about politics; and in 2006, 11 percent went to alternative news sites such as AlterNet.org or NewsMax.com, while about 10 percent did so in 2008. The frequency of usage of blogs as a source of information is particularly striking. Blogs are perhaps the quintessential example of a biased or one-sided information site and while those percentages are not a majority they are not insignificant.

Table 2.6.   Frequency of Usage of One-Sided Sites

	Pew 2006	
	Count	Percentage
Candidates' Sites	138	20.8
Issue-Oriented Sites	182	27.5
Blogs	148	22.4
Alternative News Sites	73	11.0
Number of Cases	662	
	Pew 2008	
Obama's Site	400	33.2
McCain's Site	284	23.5
Issue-Oriented Sites	272	22.6
Blogs	280	23.2
Alternative News Sites	114	9.5
Number of Cases	1206	

Note: Data come from the Pew Internet & American Life Project, November 2006 and 2008 Post-Election Tracking Surveys.

THE INTERNET AND ELECTIONS

In chapters 7 and 8, we move from analysis of the impact of the Internet on public opinion and behavior to exploring its effects on elections. First, we theorize about the changing nature of campaign finance as a result of the Internet and then we estimate the effectiveness of campaigning on the Internet. In chapter 7, we argue that the Internet is changing the necessary fundamental strategy candidates must employ for successful fundraising. The rationale for the support for campaign finance reform has been the influence of moneyed interests. Large interest groups buy access, and ultimately influence, by raising large sums of money and funneling it directly and indirectly toward campaigns. Candidates are beholden to the interests that can marshal the most resources, both monetarily and through volunteer networks. The use of the Internet changes the dynamic in two ways. Initially, it allows candidates to bypass the traditional fundraising networks and it allows candidates to reach interested volunteers directly, lessening the importance of volunteers supplied by interest groups. In exploring this effect, we use supporting existing statistics and not original data.

We return to a more empirical model in chapter 8 to estimate the influence of candidates' campaign websites on electoral success. We model how a successful web campaign is related to the number of votes a candidate actually receives. To measure and test the web as a campaign tool, we use online measures. Web presence is measured using the Google PageRank of the campaign webpage of each of the candidates in the sample. PageRank uses the number of links to a page as an indicator of an individual page's value. It interprets a link from page A to page B as a vote, by page A, for page B. It also includes in the calculus the page that casts the vote. Votes cast by pages with higher rankings themselves are weighted more heavily.[16] PageRank allows us to approximate the concept of web presence as more than an individual popularity score, but also as a representative indicator of how much success a campaign has had in integrating its web efforts into a larger and sustained political footprint in the Internet community. PageRank is the most effective measure of this larger multifaceted conceptual understanding of web presence. The rankings of candidates' pages in this sample range from 3 to 6, with higher values indicating a greater web presence.[17] As you can see from figure 2.7, the distribution is relatively normal with a mean of 4.79 and a standard deviation of 0.73. This distribution indicates that there is a fair amount of variation. Most

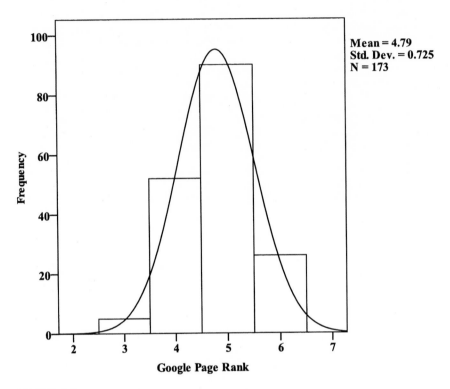

FIGURE 2.7
Distribution of Candidates' Web Presence
Source: Google, Inc.

candidates did a decent job at establishing a presence on the web, yet clearly some candidates are far more effective than others. This variance certainly provides us the opportunity to explore the influence across races.

CONCLUSION

In this chapter we laid the descriptive foundation for all the chapters that follow. In doing so, we briefly described the theoretical underpinning of each chapter, the measurement of the primary variables in each chapter, and the distribution of these variables. Again, much of the theory in this book is not necessarily novel, but its application, and primarily its tests, are. Most of the analysis that follows is multivariate and inferential, which runs counter to much of the existing research centered on the political impact of the Internet. These models can only be accurately interpreted by knowing the distribution of the variables of interest. This chapter provides this context. For instance, if the Internet is, as we assert, revolutionizing American politics, its use must be prevalent. More importantly, its use for political purposes must be pervasive. The numbers described in this chapter suggest this is the case. Further, the data described here begin to create a picture of the modern American voter. Many claim to learn from the Internet and will vote via the Internet if given the option. These voters are increasingly using social networking on the Internet and are applying it in a variety of ways to gather information. Finally, the data described in this chapter suggest that candidates are campaigning on the Internet to help win votes and elections. Taken in its entirety, the data described in this chapter lay the foundation for our argument that the Internet is changing the dynamic of how politics and campaigns operate in the United States. The revolution is just beginning.

3

The Digital Political Public

Information Gathering, Political Knowledge, and the Digital Divide

In all states, the operation of government and its relationship to its citizens is not static over time, but can be understood as being constantly in motion and evolving. The United States, like every nation, has had significant moments of societal evolution or even revolution. Perhaps one of the most important is the dawning of the media age and its impact on the way people gather information about politics. Considerable efforts have focused on the differences between print and broadcast media (Delli Carpini and Keeter 1996; Neuman, Just, and Crigler 1992; Moy and Pfau 2000). In this chapter, we expand this analysis beyond the media age into the interactive Internet society. We contend that there are lower costs associated with using the Internet to gather information than with traditional sources, and as a result, individuals who use the Internet have greater opportunities to develop knowledge about politics. Further, we argue that the disparity between the "haves" and "have-nots" when it comes to use of the Internet (*the digital divide*) may exacerbate the knowledge gap that already exists. In the end, this could shift the very foundation of American politics, as a predictable and pervasive dichotomy in knowledge about one's government creates a foundational strain on effective participation in democracy.

After reviewing the literature centered, first, on how people gather information and obtain knowledge about politics, and second, on the digital divide, our analysis utilizes survey data from both a national sample and a sample of college students to focus on a few specific questions. They are as follows: 1) Relative to traditional news sources including television, newspapers, radio, and magazines, how many people use the Internet as their primary source of news, and specifically, who are these people? 2) What types of things are people doing on the Internet to gather political information and who is doing so most? And finally, we answer the larger question: 3) Is the Internet contributing to the development of a more sophisticated public?

Our initial review of the data paints a shifting but important image of online America. In broad strokes, Internet use is growing but not pervasive. While use of the Internet as a source of news is rising, it has yet to surpass television as the most common source. In addition, a familiar socioeconomic division is readily apparent. The results offered here tell a story of the "haves" and "have-nots." The more educated, the more affluent, and the non-minorities are using the Internet to gather political information at higher rates. Yet, there are some indicators in the data to suggest that the traditional cleavages may not be dominant in the long term. The penetration of Internet usage in the Student Data provides some basis to suggest that education and a generational change may trump cleavages associated with race and income.

The data also provide us with a measure of the types of Internet usage in which people are engaging, giving texture and depth to the picture. People use the Internet to gather information in a variety of ways including reading news, viewing candidate websites, checking the accuracy of claims, reading blogs, and viewing videos. While the use of the Internet is certainly not limited to political purposes, the growing use of the Internet for obtaining political information is evident. The combination of the increasing use of the Internet to gather political knowledge, and the current socioeconomic divisions between those who use the Internet and those who do not, provides a foundation to suggest that the Internet may currently be widening the knowledge gap between the haves and have-nots.

We contend that this is more than a simple testable difference in the level of political knowledge between the rich and the poor. The result of lowered costs associated with gathering information via the Internet relative to other sources creates an ongoing and fundamental shift in the electorate. Those with Internet access can meet, discuss, plan, exchange ideas, and focus agendas, with little to no cost, from their homes. They can more effectively support their political candidates and organize their electorate. Those without access have far higher costs of organization and distribution. The costs are disproportionately lowered for the haves; thus, the already existing gap is widened by making it easier to obtain information for some. Simply, the Internet presents an opportunity for learning that does translate into more knowledge, and it does so unevenly. Those who are already expected to be more politically sophisticated are becoming even more so. As a result, the voting electorate is being tilted in a direction that will favor the most advantaged in ways not seen in the modern era.

GATHERING INFORMATION AND DEVELOPING KNOWLEDGE ABOUT GOVERNMENT AND POLITICS

There is little argument that the Internet is altering the fundamental nature of how ideas are communicated in society (Mossberger, Tolbert, and Stansbury 2003). In increasing not only the availability of information but the speed with which it is distributed to the public, the Internet continues to alter the nature and scope of public discourse. During the war in Yugoslavia, the Internet was used to constantly and rapidly disseminate information worldwide, not only on behalf of the Serbs, but also on behalf of the otherwise unheard-of Kosovars, even amidst the bombing campaign by NATO (Allison 2002). With the power to reach across the globe in seconds, the Internet is as revolutionary to communication as the telegraph and later the radio were (Klotz 2004; Steele and Stein 2002). With information so readily available, the cost associated with gathering it is significantly decreased. It is no longer necessary to buy a paper or be available at a certain time to watch a news program or listen to a radio show. Also, as highlighted with the Yugoslavian example, information from multiple perspectives is readily available. One might expect that with these lowered costs the public may become more informed. Simply, learning about politics is made easier with this technological innovation. If this theory is indeed true, it has likely positive implications for democracy.

While democratic theory has never been specific about how informed individuals need to be to fulfill the obligations of effective citizenship, most would agree that at a minimum one must have a basic understanding of government functions and of differences between candidates' policy agendas and between the parties they represent. The public will be unable to cast its ballots wisely without such an understanding. Unfortunately, more than half a century of empirical research has left the distinct impression that voters' knowledge about politics and how government works is limited (Campbell et al. 1960; Converse 1964; Popkin 1991). The advent of the Internet may ultimately reduce this deficiency by making the information more readily accessible to a larger number of people. Research that has looked at this issue suggests that the Internet may increase voter information surrounding elections, and in turn, may stimulate increased participation (Tolbert and McNeal 2003). Much of the reason that people are uninformed could be attributed to the costs associated with gathering information. The Internet lowers costs by simplifying the process by which information is obtained. Further, costs are lowered by having the information available at the convenience of the consumer.

There is growing evidence that Internet users are starting to discard more traditional media like newspapers (Lupia and Baird 2003). There are reasons to believe the Internet may be a more dynamic and significant source of information than the traditional media. The Internet is much more diverse in the way it purveys information than newspapers, magazines, radio, or television. Newspapers and magazines use primarily the written word in combination with photographic images, while television and radio rely primarily on the spoken word with images (both still and moving). On the other hand, the Internet has all of the above. Further, the Internet has the more in-depth, factually-rich information typically associated with newspapers (Delli Carpini and Keeter 1996; Graber 2006) and the sound-bite image-based style consistent with television news (Graber 2001, 2006).

In addition, the Internet provides the opportunity to explore sources that are significantly more in-depth than newspapers. The writers do not have the same page limitations. The Internet also allows for the interactive exchange of information in chat rooms, e-mail, blogs, and comment boards. In a very real sense, the Internet has all of the advantages and uses of the traditional sources, and includes an interactive networking function that allows users to involve themselves in ways previously unknown. Further, this usage is readily available on demand from the privacy of a home or office. Of course, the reliability of this information can be suspect (as can traditional media coverage), but nonetheless, this exchange encourages people to check for themselves, with the tools to confirm or reject ideas at hand. More directly, if learning takes place from reading newspapers and television, and the Internet provides those same modes of information supply plus far more, we should expect Internet use to have a greater effect on knowledge than either traditional source individually or together.

Some studies have suggested that voters learn more from reading newspapers than from watching television news programs and, in fact, the latter adds little or nothing to one's knowledge of candidates' positions (Berkowitz and Pritchard 1989; Choi and Becker 1987; Patterson 1980; Patterson and McClure 1976; Robinson and Levy 1986; Weaver and Drew 1993). Others indicate that TV news may be a meaningful source of knowledge after all (Bartels 1993; Chaffee and Schleuder 1986; Chaffee, Zhao, and Leshner 1994; Graber 1988, 2001; McLeod et al. 1996; Neuman, Just, and Crigler 1992; Weaver and Drew 1995, 2001; Zhao and Bleske 1995).[1] Of course, not everyone agrees. In their landmark study of the 1972 election, Patterson and McClure (1976, p. 54; also see Robinson and Levy 1986) conclude that television news "may be fascinating. It may be highly entertaining. But it is simply not informative."

The question that remains is, "Do people learn more about politics and government from the Internet than traditional media sources?" While research has demonstrated that a significant amount of learning about candidates takes place during election campaigns (Ansolabehere and Iyengar 1995; Alvarez 1997; Bartels 1993; Berelson, Lazarsfeld, and McPhee 1954; Buchanan 1991; Franklin 1991; Patterson 1980; Patterson and McClure 1976), it is less certain about the extent to which different media such as newspapers, television news, and now, the Internet are contributing to learning and knowledge. That said, Mossberger, Tolbert, and McNeal (2008) do find evidence of a stronger relationship between online news consumption and political knowledge than traditional media consumption and political knowledge. We seek to expand on this finding by exploring not only the effects of traditional media consumption versus Internet media consumption but by also examining the relationship between the magnitude of Internet media consumption and political knowledge.[2] To our knowledge no research has examined whether heightened political information gathering on the Internet will stimulate political knowledge.[3]

WHO'S USING THE INTERNET?

The Internet provides a learning advantage for users. As noted above, users have unprecedented access to an interactive social and political environment. If gathering information about politics on the Internet does, in fact, stimulate learning more than traditional avenues of gathering information, it suggests that the Internet users are likely to become more able to engage the political system and are therefore advantaged in their efforts to influence policy outcomes. Based on the literature that explores the "digital divide" (Gainous and Wagner 2007; Mossberger, Tolbert, and Stansbury 2003; Rainie and Bell 2004), we expect this to be a significant source of political evolution. We propose that the Internet has transformed how people get information and engage with each other, and consistent with the digital divide literature, this change is currently affecting some groups more than others. Specifically, access to and use of the Internet across demographic lines including education, income, race, gender, and age typically tells a story of the haves and have-nots.[4]

Though on its face this division is about access and opportunity, it is more complex in application. The digital divide in the United States is best understood by looking at it across three dimensions: 1) Access to the Internet; 2) Quality of equipment and connection; and 3) Technological skills. There is evidence of a have and have-not divide across all three dimensions. Most evidence on the digital divide focuses on access (see Chadwick 2006), or the availability of a computer with an Internet connection. In the 1990s the U.S. government began to take note of the disparities in access to the Internet across education, income, race, gender, geography, and age. The Department of Commerce's National Telecommunications and Information Administration (NTIA) produced several reports that highlighted these disparities. The educated, more affluent, and non-minority populations were more likely to have access. These reports spawned several government responses. Perhaps the most notable was the $2.25 billion e-rate program which subsidized access in rural areas and public schools.

During George W. Bush's tenure this policy agenda diminished. In 2002 the NTIA released a more promising report that suggested the divide was significantly decreasing. This conclusion was supportable in the report since access was defined too broadly by including access from all locations. Being able to go somewhere other than your home for Internet access is not the same as accessing the Internet from home. Offsite access has a higher cost in time and transportation, so we should expect a divide in usage to persist if home access is still less prevalent for the have-nots. Other data including those from the Pew Internet and Life Project 2004 (Rainie and Bell 2004) and a survey done by Kent State University (Mossberger, Tolbert, and Stansbury 2003) paint another picture, clearly indicating that a divide still exists across demographics when it comes to home access.

Most research fails to explore the gap when it comes to the quality of equipment and connection. We are unaware of any research that looks specifically at the disparity between the quality of computing equipment, but research has explored the pervasiveness of homes with broadband connections. The evidence suggests that the broadband divide is consistent with the access one (Chadwick 2006). As should be expected, homes with higher incomes, younger inhabitants, and in non-rural areas tend to have broadband connections at higher rates. This can be explained as a result of the financial cost incurred to carry a broadband connection. There is likely a similar divide in the quality of equipment where the have-nots are more apt to have older, slower, and cheaper equipment. Slower connections reduce the usefulness of the Internet, though they do not make it of no use. Yet, those with the best equipment and the fastest connections are the most able to use the advantages that the Internet provides. These users, especially those with the best connections, are more likely to rely on the Internet for news than on traditional sources (Horrigan and Rainie 2002). The cost of gathering information is lowered by having a faster connection and equipment. Thus, if more knowledge is gained by gathering information via the Internet, those with faster connections and equipment should be acquiring more knowledge than those without.

Based on the evidence that there is a digital divide when it comes to both access and the quality of equipment, it is reasonable to expect that the have-nots also possess fewer computer skills. Research confirms this expectation. Mossberger and her colleagues (2003) find that there is a divide in basic skills across education, age, income, race, and ethnicity. Once again, having fewer skills increases the cost of gathering information on the Internet. As socio-economics predicts online skills, this traditional measure continues to have predictive value (Krueger 2006). As a result, the have-nots will develop less knowledge than their counterparts if more knowledge is, in fact, acquired by relying on the Internet versus traditional sources.

Moving beyond how people gather information and obtain knowledge about politics, we take the next step and look to measure the impact the Internet is having on political learning across demographic groups. We propose three hypotheses: 1) Consistent with the literature, we expect to be able to identify a have and have-not divide in Internet use; 2) We also expect there to be a have and have-not divide in levels of political knowledge; and 3) We expect Internet use to be positively related to political knowledge. The results confirm these expectations. Based on the combination of these results, we argue that the Internet is creating a divided and ultimately dissimilar electorate by contributing to an exacerbated knowledge gap between the haves and have-nots. It is an evolving digital political world for some, and a conventional and far less engaging and enlightening world for many others.

METHODS

The analysis in this chapter includes a variety of descriptive statistics, cross-tabulations, difference in means tests, and regression models. While the primary objective is to look for differences across the have and have-not divide and for the effect of Internet use on knowledge, we also explore differences across traditional political variables, such as general attentiveness to public affairs and party identification, to provide a foundation for understanding the political implications of Internet use within society. We are not the first to suggest that the Internet stimulates knowledge (see Brundidge and Rice 2009), but again the primary contribution of this book is that we offer empirical evidence and test theory in a new way. In this chapter we, first, explore the reasons people go online for news. Second, we compare results across datasets regarding how respondents get most of their news. Third, we compare results centered on who is more likely to use the Internet for news across demographics, political party identification, and attentiveness to public affairs. Fourth, we highlight the different ways people are using the Internet to gather political information across both datasets. Fifth, using both datasets, we provide tests of who is using the Internet to gather political information most often. Sixth, we construct separate models of political information gathering on the Internet as a function of whether or not the Internet is one's primary source of news, level of attentiveness to public affairs, party identification, and demographics, and compare results. Seventh, using only the Student Survey Data, we test for differences across demographics in how much respondents claim to learn from a variety of political sources on the Internet.[5] Eighth, again using only the Student Data, we test for a knowledge gap across levels of Internet political information gathering, the claim to learn from the Internet, respondents' primary source of news, and demographics.[6] Finally, we conclude with a model of political knowledge as a function of levels of Internet political information gathering, the claim to learn from the Internet, respondents' primary source of news, and demographics. Justification for all the choices made in these models follows along with the description of the operationalization of all variables used here. In combination, all of these tests allow us to address our primary research questions while also providing extra descriptive and foundational information.

ANALYSIS

Before moving to the larger questions concerning the nature of the population that uses the Internet, and the purposes as well as benefits inured to them, we will analyze the antecedent question concerning the reasons people claim to use the Internet. These results provide a framework for understanding the impact of Internet use as a going concern. We assert that the costs associated with gathering information via the Internet, including time and effort, are lower than those with traditional sources of information. Hence, because information is more readily available, people who rely on the Internet should be more politically sophisticated or at least have more knowledge. The findings presented later confirm this expectation.

The results in table 3.1 indicate that the primary reason people give for going online is the lowered cost to them in the time and effort necessary for gathering or obtaining information. Respondents in the Student Data were given six response options when asked why they go online for news, and of those six options, the first, "because getting information online is more convenient," was selected by over half of the total respondents (51.5 percent). For the remaining options, 23.6 percent said it was due to the wider range of

Table 3.1. Why People Go Online for News

	Count	Percentage
More Convenient	343	51.5
Wider Range of Viewpoints	157	23.6
More In Depth	51	7.7
More Entertaining	33	5.0
Don't Use Internet for News	60	9.0
Other	22	3.3
Number of Cases	666	100.0 %

Note: Data come from a 2008 survey of college students at the University of Louisville and Florida Atlantic University.

viewpoints, 7.7 percent because of more in-depth information, and 5 percent because it is more entertaining. The rest claimed they don't go online to get news and information, or selected the "other" response. While this evidence does not tell us if gathering information via the Internet stimulates more knowledge than other ways, it is increasingly clear that the Internet has a draw for students as an increasingly efficient means to gather information. Though the Internet is growing as a source of news, and its use among students is driven in part by its ability to effectively provide news to that demographic, the pervasiveness of this type of convenience driving usage outside the Student Data is less clear.

When the analysis is divided by traditional divisions in the population, the distribution of use tells another story. Initially, we might expect those who are more attentive to public affairs to be more likely to use the Internet as their primary source of news. While there is some support for this notion, it is limited. The results in table 3.2 do show a slight pattern where people who are more attentive are more likely to claim that the Internet is their primary source of news in the Pew Data, but a chi-squared test of cell independence suggests that this pattern is not significant. Yet, this pattern is significant in the Student Data with the pattern being quite striking. More than 35 percent of those who claimed to pay attention to public affairs most of the time rely primarily on the Internet for news relative to only roughly 8 percent in the Pew Data. If there is, indeed, a knowledge gap between those who are more attentive and those who are not, and if those who are more attentive rely on the Internet, the lower costs associated with gathering information on the Internet could further exacerbate the gap.

When viewed by a partisan division the data again show an interesting pattern. Differences in partisan usage do appear to be significant in the Pew Data but are only slightly measurable in the Student Data. In the 2006 Pew Data, Independents were slightly more likely than Republicans and Republicans were slightly more likely than Democrats to use the Internet as their primary source of news. In the 2008 Pew Data, Independents again were slightly ahead of both parties, but the differences between Republicans and Democrats were insignificant. Comparatively, in the Student Data, Independents were substantially more likely to rely on the Internet than both Republicans and Democrats who were, as in the 2008 Pew Data, not significantly different. Interestingly, over 30 percent of Independent students claimed that the

Internet is their primary source relative to only just over 10 percent in the Pew Data. Independent students may prefer the Internet because information about alternative positions is more prevalent and accessible as compared to traditional sources. Traditional sources are increasingly marketing themselves towards competing, yet widely held, ideological centers, making alternative information a less profitable commodity.

Among well-studied voting demographics that represent the digital divide, the expected differences are evident in the Pew Data, but not in the Student Data. In the Pew Data, younger people were more likely than older people to rely on the Internet as their primary news source. Though there are substantial increases in the use of the Internet as a primary news source over all age groups in the 2008 Pew Data, the trend is similar: younger people are using the online resources in greater numbers. However, it is worth noting that the growth in use by older Americans is diluting this trend. In 2006, only 7 percent of Americans forty to forty-nine used the Internet as their primary news source. This doubled in two years to 14 percent. While the percentage of forty- to forty-nine-year-olds does not match the younger groups in either 2006 or 2008, the numbers were closer in 2008. This is not so in the Student Data but this is likely a result of the lack of variation in the age variable in the Student Data. Both education and income are significant in the Pew Data; the analysis was not performed using the Student Data because students are the educated (or are at least in the process of becoming so) and most are yet to be earning significant incomes. Instead of testing for differences across income in the Student Data, we explore differences across students' claim about their parents' finances, and the chi-squared test of independence suggests that there is no relationship.

As for differences across race, the findings are distinctive. While the chi-squared test is significant in the 2006 Pew Data, there was no major difference between whites, blacks, and Latinos (Latinos are slightly less likely to claim the Internet is their primary news source). Rather, the significant finding is driven by a massive difference between these three races and those who are categorized as "other race." Of those in this category, 16 percent claimed that the Internet is their primary news source while whites were at 7.4 percent, blacks at 7.1 percent, and Latinos at 5.7 percent. Those who claimed to be another race were most likely from areas in Asia or the Middle East. The differences in the 2008 Pew Data are far more striking. All races show an increase

Table 3.2. Who Is Using the Internet as Their Primary Source of News?

	Pew Data				Student Data	
	2006		2008		2008	
	Int %	T.S. %	Int %	T.S. %	Int %	T.S. %
Civic Attentiveness						
Never (Volunteered)	4.2	95.8 (24)	—	—	—	—
Hardly at all	4.8	95.2 (227)	—	—	10.7	89.3 (84)
Only now and then	6.0	94.0 (284)	—	—	15.3	84.7 (137)
Some of the time	7.9	92.1 (720)	—	—	20.7	79.3 (237)
Most of the time	8.3	91.7 (1307)	—	—	35.6	64.4 (208)
χ^2		0.30				0.00
Party Identification						
Republican	8.1	91.9 (688)	10.8	89.2 (601)	20.9	79.1 (177)
Democrat	5.5	94.5 (1138)	9.3	90.7 (867)	21.0	79.0 (310)
Independent	10.2	89.8 (736)	13.0	87.0 (655)	30.3	69.7 (119)
χ^2		0.00	0.08		0.10	
Age						
18–29	18.0	82.0 (395)	23.3	76.7 (202)	22.7	77.3 (639)
30–39	11.4	88.6 (378)	20.0	80.0 (270)	35.0	65.0 (20)
40–49	6.9	93.1 (465)	14.0	86.0 (379)	25.0	75.0 (4)
50–59	5.7	94.3 (506)	9.8	90.2 (429)	0.0	100.0 (1)
60 and up	2.3	97.7 (818)	4.2	95.8 (843)	0.0	100.0 (2)
χ^2		0.00	0.00		0.63	
Education						
None or grades 1–8	0.0	100.0 (56)	2.1	97.9 (48)	—	—
H.S. Incomplete	2.3	97.7 (175)	1.6	98.4 (127)	—	—
H.S. Graduate	4.7	95.3 (758)	5.1	94.9 (622)	—	—
Tech School	2.5	97.5 (81)	3.8	96.2 (80)	—	—
Some College/Assoc.	7.7	92.3 (625)	13.7	86.3 (518)	—	—
College Graduate	11.9	88.1 (539)	17.8	82.2 (426)	—	—
Post-Graduate	12.2	87.8 (328)	15.2	84.8 (302)	—	—
χ^2		0.00	0.00			
Income						
Less than $10,000	4.8	95.2 (145)	3.3	96.7	—	—
$10,000–$20,000	4.4	95.6 (228)	5.5	94.5	—	—
$20,000–$30,000	3.7	96.3 (324)	4.9	95.1	—	—
$30,000–$40,000	6.1	93.9 (409)	6.6	93.4	—	—
$40,000–$50,000	4.6	95.4 (390)	11.2	88.8	—	—
$50,000–$75,000	7.9	92.1 (454)	10.2	89.8	—	—
$75,000–$100,000	11.4	88.6 (290)	19.3	80.7	—	—
$100,000 or More	16.5	83.5 (322)	21.1	78.9	—	—
χ^2		0.00	0.00			
Parents' Finances						
Poor	—	—	—	—	32.8	67.2 (58)
Middle	—	—	—	—	23.3	76.7 (407)
Well Off	—	—	—	—	19.4	80.6 (201)
χ^2					0.10	

Table 3.2. *(continued)*

	Pew Data				Student Data	
	2006		2008		2008	
	Int %	T.S. %	Int %	T.S. %	Int %	T.S. %
Race						
White	7.4	92.6 (2059)	10.7	89.3 (1712)	24.2	75.8 (491)
Black	7.1	92.9 (252)	8.0	92.0 (212)	18.7	81.3 (75)
Latino	5.7	94.3 (157)	12.4	87.6 (129)	15.9	84.1 (44)
Asian	7.9	92.1(38)	23.3	76.7 (30)	28.6	71.4 (21)
Other	16.0	84.0 (94)	17.5	82.5 (40)	20.0	80.0 (35)
χ^2		0.01	0.07		0.56	
Gender						
Male	9.2	90.8 (1223)	13.9	86.1(1003)	26.2	73.8 (321)
Female	6.0	94.0 (1339)	8.2	91.8 (1120)	20.0	80.0 (345)
χ^2		0.00	0.00		0.06	
Number of Cases	2562	2123	666			

Note: Data come from the Pew Internet & American Life Project, November 2006 and 2008 Post-Election Tracking Surveys, and a 2008 survey of college students at the University of Louisville and Florida Atlantic University. Int % refers to the percentage of respondents who use the Internet and T.S. % is the percentage who use traditional sources such as television, radio, newspapers, and magazines (and other for the Student Data). The total number of cases for each row category is in parentheses. χ^2 refers to the probability that there is not cell dependence across each cross-tabulation.

in using the Internet as their primary source of news, but the magnitude of the increases differs substantially. Asian Americans moved from 8 percent in 2006 to 23 percent in 2008. Latinos rose to 12.4 percent in 2008 from 5.7 percent in 2006. Caucasians had modest growth from 7.4 percent to 10.7, while African Americans lagged, moving up less than a percentage point from 7.1 to 8 percent in the 2008 data. The Pew Data supports the notion that there are still substantial social divides in the distribution and use of the Internet.

While there were racial measures and response categories in the Student Data, the test results suggest that there is no relationship across race. Nonetheless, it is worth noting, as in the case of the Pew Data, Asian Americans are leading the adoption of the Internet as a primary news source. Of those who identified themselves as Asian, 28.6 percent, the highest percentage in the data, claimed that the Internet is their primary source of election news. Finally, there does appear to be a difference across gender in both datasets. Males were more likely than females to claim that the Internet is their main news source (9.2 to 6 percent in the 2006 Pew Data, 13.9 to 8.2 in the 2008 Pew Data, and 26.2 to 20 percent in the Student Data).

The divisions in who uses the Internet are interesting, but the importance of that usage in the political context is the primary inquiry. The Internet lowers the cost of gathering information, but the variety of ways people can use to find and explore political information is significant and suggests different types of learning and comprehension. We test across demographics concerning how much political information gathering on the Internet is actually happening. There are some stark differences across both demographics and other traditional political variables when it comes to gathering political information via the Internet. We assert that these differences provide evidence of a digital divide, and again, argue that the costs of gathering this information are lowered for these groups that use the Internet. Interestingly, the differences that show up here are primarily present in the Pew Data, suggesting that youth and education can alleviate the traditional have and have-not cleavages. The tests provided in table 3.3 are differences of means tests based on the indices of political information gathering described in chapter 2 that were constructed

Table 3.3. Differences in Political Information Gathering on the Internet across Independent Variables

	Pew Data				Student Data	
	2006		2008		2008	
	Mean	P	Mean	P	Mean	P
Primary News Source						
Internet	8.31(3.46)		9.31(3.38)		2.97(1.65)	
Traditional Sources	7.13(3.51)	0.00	7.53(3.42)	0.00	1.82(1.45)	0.00
Civic Attentiveness						
Hardly at all	4.89(3.48)		—		0.79(0.97)	
Only now and then	5.38(3.22)		—		1.40(1.25)	
Some of the time	6.78(3.16)		—		1.99(1.36)	
Most of the time	7.97(3.55)	0.00	—	—	3.18(1.50)	0.00
Party Identification						
Republican	7.27(3.65)		7.59(3.47)		1.96(1.47)	
Democrat	7.54(3.43)		6.88(3.97)		2.36(1.67)	
Independent	7.39(3.55)	0.72	7.87(3.40)	0.01	2.01(1.41)	0.01
Age						
18–29	6.78(3.48)		7.96(3.57)		2.07(1.57)	
30–39	7.80(3.43)		7.97(3.40)		2.89(1.61)	
40–49	7.74(3.60)		8.08(3.57)		1.70(1.76)	
50–59	7.36(3.63)		7.50(3.46)		0.20(0.00)	
60 and up	7.22(3.45)	0.13	—	0.00	2.00(1.41)	0.12

Table 3.3. *(continued)*

	Pew Data				Student Data	
	2006		2008		2008	
	Mean	P	Mean	P	Mean	P
Education						
None or grades 1–8			6.67(3.79)		—	
H.S. Incomplete	6.75(2.90)		4.73(3.15)		—	
H.S. Graduate	6.07(3.63)		6.97(3.36)		—	
Tech School	5.88(3.53)		7.30(3.39)		—	
Some College/Assoc.	7.56(3.62)		7.81(3.51)		—	
College Graduate	7.55(3.48)		8.50(3.48)		—	
Post-Graduate	7.93(3.35)	0.00	8.49(3.33)	0.00	—	—
Income						
Less than $10,000	5.67(2.90)		6.94(3.11)		—	
$10,000–$20,000	6.89(3.96)		8.07(3.28)		—	
$20,000–$30,000	7.03(4.07)		6.42(3.26)		—	
$30,000–$40,000	6.62(3.31)		7.55(3.88)		—	
$40,000–$50,000	6.84(3.77)		7.15(3.42)		—	
$50,000–$75,000	7.14(3.37)		7.92(3.43)		—	
$75,000–$100,000	7.95(3.29)		8.20(3.45)		—	
$100,000 or more	8.12(3.55)	0.01	8.77(3.38)	0.00	—	—
Parents' Finances						
Poor	—		—		2.46(1.68)	
Middle	—		—		2.08(1.61)	
Well Off	—	—	—	—	2.01(1.46)	0.16
Race						
White	7.42(3.54)		7.99(3.51)		2.12(1.60)	
Black	7.45(3.51)		8.39(3.41)		2.07(1.50)	
Latino	6.17(3.29)		6.47(3.32)		1.78(1.44)	
Asian	5.67(1.63)		7.70(3.36)		1.74(1.20)	
Other	10.00(3.07)	0.01	7.47(3.64)	0.86	2.29(1.77)	0.49
Gender						
Male	7.37(3.65)		8.12(3.52)		2.08(1.65)	
Female	7.46(3.40)	0.75	7.79(3.45)	0.15	2.10(1.51)	0.89
Number of Cases	657		918		666	

Note: Data come from the Pew Internet & American Life Project, November 2006 and 2008 Post-Election Tracking Surveys, and a 2008 survey of college students at the University of Louisville and Florida Atlantic University. P represents the probability that we cannot reject the null hypothesis that there is no difference in the magnitude of political Internet use across all above independent variables (T-tests for dichotomous independent variables and one-way ANOVA tests—between groups—for ordinal and non-dichotomous nominal independent variables). Standard deviations for each are in parentheses. *Traditional sources* refers to television, radio, newspapers, and magazines. There was only one case for none or grades 1–8 so we excluded it.

from all of the items contained in table 2.3.[7] For the Pew Data (2006 and 2008), t-tests suggest that those whose primary source of news is the Internet use the Internet to gather political information much more than those who rely on traditional sources. T-tests also suggest that males use it no less than females. Additionally, one-way ANOVA tests indicate that those who are more attentive to public affairs used the Internet to gather information more than the less attentive in 2006. There was not a measure of attentiveness in the 2008 Pew Data. The tests also show that age is not a significant factor in 2006 ($p = 0.13$). It is important to remember that these data reflect differences among those who claim to have used the Internet to obtain information about the elections. These questions were only asked of them. On the other hand, differences across age were significant in 2008. Those in the forty- to forty-nine-year-old category led all age groups. Blacks and whites used the Internet to gather information more than other races in 2006, though the differences between races in the 2008 data declined sharply, making the distinctions insignificant in those data. Finally, for the most part, the educated and those with higher incomes used it more than their respective counterparts. If Internet use does indeed stimulate knowledge, it would appear that this phenomenon will be more pronounced for certain groups, though the effects across traditional cleavages like race are mixed.

As noted above, the findings are not all consistent across datasets. None of the tests for difference across standard demographics (age, race, gender, and parents' finances) are significant in the Student Data. This does not detract from our theory but rather suggests that education and youth may eventually alleviate the disparities and the public as a whole may become more informed. While the demographic findings are not the same, the findings for primary news source and attentiveness are consistent with the Pew Data. Interestingly, there are significant differences across party identification in the Student Data and the results are the opposite of those in the Pew Data (although the differences in the Pew Data are not significant). Those who identify themselves as Democrats were most likely to gather information via the Internet. Consistent with the Pew Data, Independents were second, and opposite of the Pew Data, Republicans were the least likely to gather information from the Internet.

Generally, these effects hold up in a multivariate setting. The results contained in table 3.4 suggest that, for both datasets, one of the strongest predictors in this model of how much people use the Internet to gather political

Table 3.4. Models of Political Information Gathering on the Internet

	Pew Data		Student Data
	2006	2008	2008
Internet Primary News Source	0.74*	0.85*	1.01*
	(0.17)	(0.14)	(0.17)
Civic Attentiveness	0.58*	—	1.14*
	(0.10)	—	(0.08)
Republican	−0.11	−0.26*	−0.31*
	(0.15)	(0.13)	(0.16)
Age	−0.06	−0.10*	−0.28
	(0.06)	(0.04)	(0.21)
Black	0.13	0.22	0.22
	(0.27)	(0.23)	(0.22)
Latino	−0.28	−1.03**	0.23
	(0.33)	(0.43)	(0.28)
Female	0.18	−0.07	0.31*
	(0.14)	(0.12)	(0.14)
Education	0.11*	0.21*	—
	(0.06)	(0.04)	—
Income/Parents' Finances	0.09*	0.12*	0.06
	(0.04)	(0.04)	(0.12)
−2 Log Likelihood	3093.18	4032.00	2341.37
Nagelkerke Pseudo R^2	0.12	0.11	0.34
Number of Cases	657	918	666

Note: Data come from the Pew Internet & American Life Project, November 2006 and August 2008 Post-Election Tracking Surveys, and a 2008 survey of college students at the University of Louisville and Florida Atlantic University. Table entries are ordered logit estimates with associated standard errors in parentheses. *$p \le 0.05$.

information is whether or not their primary news source is the Internet or more traditional sources such as television, radio, newspapers, or magazines. This effect holds up when controlling for other factors that also influence how much information gathering in which one is engaging. While we have to be careful of making a direct comparison of the magnitude of this effect to other variables in the model because the models do not have the exact same specifications, the effect increased from the 2006 to the 2008 data. Additionally, the other variables that are dichotomous do not even come close to this strong of an effect (with the exception of Latino in 2008), though civic attentiveness also has a strong and positive effect favoring information gathering on the Internet in the 2006 model.

Nonetheless, several other variables in the Pew Data are significant as well. Consistent with the means tests described above, those who are more attentive to public affairs (in 2006) are younger (in 2008), more educated, have higher incomes, and tend to use the Internet to gather political information more. This holds true in both the data from 2006 and 2008. The 2008 data does present one significant difference. In 2008, being a Latino decreased the likelihood of using the Internet for political information gathering. Interestingly, the party identification, non-Latino race categories, and gender effects apparent in the means tests do not hold up in either the 2006 or 2008 models. This suggests that the variance explained by these variables can actually be accounted for by the significant variables in the model. The model seems to perform fairly well overall. The Nagelkerke Pseudo R^2 suggests that approximately 12 percent (2006) or 11 percent (2008) of the variance in the dependent variable is accounted for by the variables in the model. On the other hand, while the R^2 is roughly 0.34 in the Student Data model of political information gathering, overall, it does not perform as well. This mirrors the lack of findings contained in the means tests, but there is one exception: Gender becomes significant. Females are more actively gathering information via the Internet in the student sample. Interestingly, this is in contrast with the means tests in the Pew Data. Overall, when looking at both models we can assume that the digital divide across the haves and have-nots is present in the general population, but less so among the young and educated.

The central premise of this chapter is that the costs associated with gathering information via the Internet are lowered relative to those associated with traditional sources, and as a result, those who rely on the Internet have greater opportunity to inform themselves. Further, this opportunity is more readily available for the haves as opposed to the have-nots. With this in mind, we move to the final puzzle as to whether or not learning and knowledge development is occurring for those who rely on the Internet. This analysis draws from the Student Data and utilizes two primary measures. The first is a meta-attitudinal measure of the claim by students of having obtained learning from the Internet. This is a subjective assessment from the respondents. The second is an operative measure of political knowledge that attempts to gauge respondents' basic knowledge about both the functions and players in the American political system.

While there are some informative findings when it comes to claiming to learn about presidential candidates from various sources on Internet, the results in table 3.5, overall, do not strongly address the have and have-not divide across Internet learning. First, there is no apparent race effect. Essentially, no race claimed more than the others to learn about candidates from newspaper websites, online news magazines, blogs, or candidates' websites. This finding is confirmed when looking for differences using an index of all four items.

Table 3.5.   Differences across the Claim to Learn about Presidential Candidates from Sources on the Internet

	Newspaper Sites	Online News Mags	Blogs	Candidates' Sites	Index
Race					
White	3.00	2.14	1.66	2.00	8.81
Black	2.95	2.00	1.83	1.93	8.71
Latino	2.98	2.05	1.73	1.86	8.61
Asian	2.81	2.00	1.62	1.48	7.90
Other	2.91	2.06	1.49	1.94	8.40
P-value	**0.87**	**0.72**	**0.36**	**0.19**	**0.57**
Parents' Finances					
Poor	3.14	2.45	1.79	2.14	9.52
Middle	2.96	2.09	1.65	1.97	8.67
Well Off	2.99	2.05	1.69	1.92	8.65
P-value	**0.35**	**0.02**	**0.48**	**0.33**	**0.07**
Age					
18–29	2.97	2.09	1.67	1.95	8.67
30–39	3.60	2.70	2.00	2.40	10.70
40–49	3.25	3.00	1.25	3.00	10.50
50–59	1.00	1.00	1.00	1.00	4.00
60 and up	2.50	2.00	1.50	1.50	7.50
P-value	**0.00**	**0.01**	**0.34**	**0.05**	**0.00**
Party Identification					
Strong Republican	3.11	2.20	1.80	2.13	9.24
Weak Republican	3.02	2.05	1.55	1.85	8.48
Lean Republican	2.80	2.00	1.53	1.63	7.97
Independent	2.66	1.84	1.50	1.66	7.66
Lean Democrat	3.04	2.04	1.67	2.00	8.74
Weak Democrat	2.94	2.08	1.68	1.92	8.63
Strong Democrat	3.04	2.26	1.75	2.12	9.17
P-value	**0.10**	**0.11**	**0.24**	**0.02**	**0.01**
Gender					
Male	2.95	2.13	1.67	1.94	8.69
Female	3.01	2.09	1.68	1.99	8.77
P-value	**0.43**	**0.56**	**0.87**	**0.49**	**0.72**
Number of Cases = 666					

Note: Data come from a 2008 survey of college students at the University of Louisville and Florida Atlantic University. P-values represent the probability that we cannot reject the null hypothesis that there is no difference in the magnitude of the claim to learn from the Internet across all above independent variables (T-tests for dichotomous independent variables and one-way ANOVA tests—between groups—for ordinal and non-dichotomous nominal independent variables). Traditional sources refers to television, radio, newspapers, and magazines.

Nonetheless, the mean score across all races is relatively high for newspaper websites, suggesting that most claimed to at least sometimes learn from such sites. The other sources are lower but are still near the midpoint of the scale indicating that many claimed to learn from all these sources. These distributions are consistent across all demographics.

As for differences within demographics, there are significant results across parents' finances and age, as well as party identification. Though there are significant differences as noted above, these findings don't tell us much about a have and have-not divide. For example, the significant finding across parents' finances ($p = 0.07$) for the index actually indicates that those who claimed to grow up poor were more likely to claim to learn from the Internet. Age is significant, but the findings must be qualified with the fact that the number of respondents outside the lower age brackets is so low that inferences are hazy at best. On the other hand, the findings across party identification are actually quite revealing. They indicate that the claim to learn increases as the strength of partisanship increases. Finally, there are no significant gender effects.[8]

Moving away from the subjective claim of learning through the Internet, we look for a digital divide across actual knowledge. The findings in table 3.6 are quite clear and provide solid support for the contention that there is a knowledge gap and this gap may be exacerbated by the lowered costs associated with information gathering via the Internet. Perhaps most important to this contention, a t-test shows that those who use the Internet to gather political information more frequently score higher on the political knowledge index. We used the median for political information gathering on the Internet as a cut-point. Those above the median were able to answer 2.22 of three knowledge questions correctly while those below the median only were able to get 1.67 correct. Those above the median on the claim to learn from the Internet also score significantly higher than those below the median (2.12 to 1.68 respectively). Likewise, those who indicated that the Internet is their primary source of news also scored higher on the knowledge index (2.31 to 1.86). As should be expected, those who are more attentive to civic affairs clearly score higher on the index.

We also reviewed the possibility of a knowledge gap across the haves and have-nots. First, there appears to be a clear gap across race. Whites score highest on the knowledge index followed by those who selected "other race." Subsequently, in order of knowledge are African Americans, followed by Asians,

Table 3.6. Differences in Political Knowledge across Independent Variables

	Mean	S.D.	P-value
Internet Information Gathering			
Above Median	2.22	0.89	
Below Median	1.67	0.98	0.00
Claim to Learn from Internet			
Above Median	2.12	0.91	
Below Median	1.68	1.01	0.00
Primary Source of News			
Internet	2.31	0.85	
Traditional Sources	1.86	0.99	0.00
Civic Attentiveness			
Hardly at all	1.10	0.94	
Only now and then	1.56	0.96	
Some of the time	1.96	0.88	
Most of the time	2.57	0.65	0.00
Race			
White	2.05	0.94	
Black	1.79	1.00	
Latino	1.45	1.04	
Asian	1.71	0.90	
Other	1.80	1.05	0.00
Parents' Finances			
Poor	2.05	1.00	
Middle	1.99	0.95	
Well Off	1.88	0.00	0.35
Gender			
Male	2.02	0.99	
Female	1.90	0.95	0.11
Age			
18–29	1.94	0.98	
30–39	2.45	0.69	
40–49	2.75	0.50	
50–59	3.00	0.00	
60 and up	2.50	0.71	0.04
Major			
Political Science	2.49	0.99	
Other	1.80	0.69	0.00
Total N (666)			

Note: Data come from a 2008 survey of college students at the University of Louisville and Florida Atlantic University. P-values represent the probability that we cannot reject the null hypothesis that there is no difference in the magnitude of the claim to learn from the Internet across all above independent variables (T-tests for dichotomous independent variables and one-way ANOVA tests—between groups—for ordinal and non-dichotomous nominal independent variables). Traditional sources refers to television, radio, newspapers, and magazines.

with Latinos scoring lowest. These findings are consistent with the gap across Internet use in the Pew Data discussed earlier. Thus, if Internet use and race are associated with a knowledge gap, heightened Internet use could exacerbate this gap. Second, the findings are not as clear across other demographics. Age is significant, but parents' finances and gender are not. It is important to note that this does not mean that they will not be so in a multivariate setting. In addition, we included a measure of major in school to control for those who are majoring in political science, as they should be expected to know more about politics than those majoring in other disciplines. The findings confirm this expectation.

Up to this point, the evidence presented has primarily served as a means of setting up a framework for understanding the details of how Internet use may be related to the development of political knowledge. Essentially the table has been set for the multivariate model of political knowledge in table 3.7. The results here are clear. There is a strong positive relationship between gathering political information via the Internet and political knowledge. It is important to note that this relationship is present while controlling for other important factors, such as the claim to learn from the Internet, whether or not the Internet is one's primary source of news, general civic attentiveness, the have and have-not demographics, and whether or not one is a political science major.

Table 3.7.   Model of Political Knowledge

	Estimate	S.E.	95% Confidence Intervals	
Internet Information Gathering	0.21	0.04	0.83	0.34
Learn from Internet	−0.02	0.07	−0.10	0.05
Internet Primary News Source	0.34	0.19	−0.04	0.72
Civic Attentiveness	0.77	0.10	0.59	0.96
White	0.53	0.17	0.20	0.86
Parents' Finances	−0.05	0.13	−0.30	0.20
Female	−0.11	0.15	−0.41	0.18
Age	0.44	0.27	−0.10	0.97
Political Science Major	0.78	0.20	0.40	1.17
−2 Log Likelihood	1424.63			
Nagelkerke Pseudo R^2	0.32			
Number of Cases	666			

Note: Data come from a 2008 survey of college students at the University of Louisville and Florida Atlantic University. Table entries are ordered logit estimates, associated standard errors, and 95% confidence intervals.

Controlling for these factors helps assure that the effect of gathering information via the Internet is not spurious. Of those variables, civic attentiveness is significant and positive. Race is significant indicating that whites are likely to score higher on the knowledge indicator. As one would expect, political science majors also score higher.

Perhaps the most interesting non-finding in these results is that whether or not the Internet is one's primary source of news is not a significant predictor of political knowledge. This result is counter to the findings in Mossberger, Tolbert, and McNeal (2008). They did not control for the magnitude of information gathered via the Internet. Thus, it appears that knowledge is not generated simply by choosing the Internet as one's primary source of news but rather it matters how one uses the Internet. This finding is consistent with our theory that the Internet lowers the cost of gathering information. Those who use the Internet as their primary source of news are provided the opportunity to gather information at lower costs than those who rely on traditional sources, but it not simply reliance on the Internet that drives knowledge. It is heightened information gathering that can result from reliance on the Internet that stimulates increased knowledge.

We assert that taken altogether, this model provides support to our theory that lowered costs associated with gathering information via the Internet versus traditional sources should stimulate knowledge. People who are using the Internet are increasingly more informed about politics and that knowledge provides them greater opportunity to participate and engage with the electoral system. To be left off the Internet will mean more than missing the ability to obtain entertainment; it will mean being left behind as the political discourse and knowledge sources increasingly find their way onto the Internet. As the above data illustrate, the patterns favoring certain groups are already clear.

CONCLUSION

The findings presented here suggest several things. First, the vast majority of people who go online for news do so because it is convenient. The costs are lowered relative to those associated with gathering information using traditional sources. Second, while the number of people who rely on the Internet as their primary source of news is growing, more traditional sources, especially television, are still dominant. Third, there is some variation across the haves and have-nots when it comes to who is more likely to rely on the

Internet as their primary news source, and who uses it to gather political information most. Finally, and most important to our theory in this chapter, the evidence suggests that information gathering via the Internet is positively associated with political knowledge. This empirical evidence seeks to quell debate on the influence that exists in some of the non-empirical existing work. We move from conjecture to a hard test. That said, more needs to be done to generalize these results as there are serious limitations to relying on Student Data. Nonetheless, we contend that the advent of the Internet does indeed make information more readily available and encourages a more sophisticated public but, as a result of the digital divide, this effect is more pronounced for many already advantaged groups. Yet, as the differences in the 2006 and 2008 data demonstrate, the effects of the social divides in our nation are not constant and do change.

The evidence presented here provides support to the idea that the Internet is changing the underlying calculus of the American political system. A more informed public has real and significant implications for democracy. If that informed public consists of particular groups at the expense of others, it exacerbates known cleavages and creates new ones as well. However, the contrast between the findings for the Pew Data and Student Data in this chapter suggests that the digital divide may dissipate as younger generations come of age. Perhaps the Internet could be the impetus for a more equal distribution of political sophistication among voters in the United States.

4

Balloting Online

Voting and the Internet

The use of the Internet can change how people engage the political system, as we have seen in previous chapters. However, it is not limited to the gathering of knowledge or to political communication. The Internet can become part of the electoral machinery directly. During the 2000 presidential primary election, the Arizona Democratic Party brought politics and technology together by allowing party members to use remote Internet access to vote in the Democratic presidential primary. This became the first attempt to test the viability of holding a binding election for public office in the United States on the Internet (Solop 2000). While there were no reported problems, there has been no large-scale adoption of Internet voting, though it continues to be considered especially as a limited part of the electoral process (Prevost and Schaffner 2008).

The implications of Internet voting are not well studied in the United States as it has not been adopted in any jurisdiction, though scholars have suggested some implications (Alvarez and Nagler 2001). Most of the early work was largely only in theoretical terms without a substantive explanatory model (Solop 2001). Yet, changing the mechanism and means by which people vote is markedly more significant than many understand. In this chapter, we explore the implications of moving the electoral machinery onto the Internet. Using a rational utility model (Downs 1957), we analyze just how such a change could alter the electoral landscape. Extending the economic and social cleavage analysis from chapter 3, we predict the likely demographic impact on voter turnout. We test this approach and the introduction of Internet voting using a Bayesian analysis of the aggregate Arizona voting data to assess the value of cost-benefit analysis on turnout and voting demographics in the digital age. Finally, we explore the use of the Internet for voting in other jurisdictions that was conducted more recently and compare some of their findings to our own.

In previous chapters, we have explored how the Internet helps shape public opinion by how it transmits and stores ideas, interaction, and information. Ideas are important engines for governance and help structure society. The very idea of American democracy was a compilation of ideas on governance and the distribution of power. Ideas are powerful stimuli for change. However, they are not the only ones. The mechanisms of governance are a more overt form of stimulus (see Wagner and Prior 2008). The rules that govern the voting process certainly structure the outcomes of elections (Gill and Gainous 2002). Most Americans would agree with the notion that each American is entitled to the same democratic representation, yet only a cursory review illustrates that this is not the case. The election of the president through the mal-apportioned Electoral College, and the representation in the Senate are strikingly unfair (Lee and Oppenheimer 1999). Because of the rule assigning two senators to each state regardless of population, residents in smaller states receive a greater say than their fellow citizens in larger states. As a result, the system often dictates outcomes if not policy results (Riker 1986). Even systems that appear overtly neutral can have unseen biases. In this chapter, we illustrate and measure the biases that would manifest from the adoption of the Internet as the means of voting. We will review how the Internet could change the nature of representation in the United States and the foundational balance between the branches of the American government, not by changing why we do something, but rather how we do it.

Technology is an exogenous stimulus that affects society. It can change how people engage with one another, how they work, and more directly, how they vote. Americans were exposed to the impact of electoral machinery during the 2000 election when discussions of punch-card ballots illustrated the surprising difficulty of translating the wishes of the voter to a clear and readable vote (Gillman 2003). Former vice president Al Gore, among others, received a powerful lesson concerning the impact of how we vote on who wins elections. In the absence of the punch-card ballot, Gore may very well have been elected president. While the conversation concerning the 2000 presidential election often degenerates into a familiar group of accusations concerning fraud or attempted fraud, the undeniable reality is that any mechanism favors or disadvantages voters based on individual experience and understanding. As Florida and other states have learned, no matter what mechanism is adopted, there is always a winner and a loser. What is easy and efficient for one voter may not be the same for other voters. Certainly not all voters were confused by the structure or nature of the ballot in Florida in 2000. Unfortunately for Gore, the vast majority of voters confused by the butterfly design of the ballot in Palm Beach County, Florida, were seniors and likely Gore voters (Gillman 2003).

While ideas are potent engines of change, the means to effect change can be as important as, or even work in conjunction with, new conceptual understandings of the state, as was the case with voting technology and the referendum. Nonetheless, we seek to isolate technology as a variable, because it can have a significant effect in creating change even in the absence of a conceptual shift simply by maximizing the voices of those with access and knowledge over those without. The Internet changes the means and operation of the system at a fundamental level by adding a new procedural lens to the equation. While superficially, this type of change can be seen as an ideological movement in the population, it really is nothing more than changing what we are counting and how we are counting it. By using a measure that favors one group or demographic over another, the result can be skewed to favor one outcome over another (Riker 1986).

If the change is of sufficient magnitude, the alteration alone is enough to redefine representation and politics themselves, even when the rule system defining representation and the political system remain unchanged. Technology as a stimulus can change the entire interactive dynamic between the society and the government by affecting people's behavior, and as a result, how and to what degree they engage with state institutions. If technology favors one group over another in political participation, then the end result will be a government which is more responsive to the advantaged groups, and policies will be implemented that are favorable to that group. In this chapter, we will examine how technology can be a significant stimulus as an isolated variable as well as in combination with other stimuli generated through societal change.

At first glance, the Internet would appear to be ideologically neutral and a solution to many of the problems Americans, especially Floridians, experienced during the 2000 election. Moving elections to the Internet in a process known as e-voting, or sometimes i-voting, has much to recommend it. Voting on the Internet removes long lines, avoids mistakes by poll workers, and can be done with deliberation and careful consideration from home or work. It is more convenient, and the counting should be much faster as the ballots can be tabulated as the votes are cast rather than stored and later run through machines. As an abstraction, Internet voting seems to be a very substantial improvement over traditional paper ballots and counting machines.

Yet, not everything is as it appears. This technology presents a new and potentially significant stimulus in the analysis of voting behavior. If voters regularly vote on the Internet, it may well change who votes by encouraging people with access to computers to participate and discourage others. It may change for whom people vote. Polling places are filled with signs and volunteers. In a long line voters may change their minds multiple times based on conversations with the people surrounding them, the campaign material placed around the polling place, or even based solely on an extended period to consider the vote itself. An Internet voter may be influenced by e-mail solicitations, web advertising, or none of the above if their system is well protected from unwanted or unrequested solicitations. The efficiency in time that an Internet voter will experience may by itself change the average length of deliberation a voter gives to his decision and the amount of consideration candidates are given.

While the internal deliberations of the voters are an interesting and perhaps significant influence derived from Internet voting, we will save our measures and analysis of Internet behavior for other chapters. For the purposes of this chapter, we are going to avoid the larger psychological implications of the technology and focus on the practical implications of technology and the Internet on political institutions and the resulting shifts in function and power in the institutional structure. We will explore the more direct and physical impact of this change—the measurable change, if any, in who will vote when the system is moved online. To address this puzzle, we will begin with the theoretical foundation for who votes and why. We do not change the fundamental structure of such analysis in political science. Using such theories, we will measure the impact of the technology stimulus by exploring and measuring the effect of e-voting on turnout and representation. We will empirically test the assertion that technology can affect voting turnout and results.

Using a standard Downsian rational choice voting theory, we claim that Internet voting lowers the cost of voting for certain voting demographics based upon race, age, and income. More directly, we assert that the Internet provides a means to effect an electoral cleavage and favor white voters, younger voters, and the more affluent, with those demographic groups likely having an increasing impact on elections, and ultimately on policy generated from those elections. We further contend that this electoral advantage may crystallize the growing turnout disparity between demographic groups, helping create an electorate that over-represents those most able to access and use Internet technology. Using Bayesian inferential methods and data gathered from the 2000 Arizona Democratic presidential primary, which was held in part on the Internet, combined with demographic data obtained from the 2000 census, we test the theory that technology generates a different electorate and discuss the implications of this assertion on future political coalitions. Finally, we compare our findings to recent research in other jurisdictions and consider the likely implications.

E-VOTING: ANTICIPATING THE IMPACT OF TECHNOLOGY

Over the course of American history, technology has changed to make it increasingly possible for the public to express opinions and convey those opinions to the state. The question left unanswered by the evolution of this communication technology is how this change might alter or revolutionize the nature of our political representation in the United States. This is a particularly difficult outcome to predict, as it calls for a conclusion about the combination of unforeseen technology on a construct designed with a focus on the concerns framed by a social structure that existed in the eighteenth century. Further, the addition of extensive communication technology is influenced not just by the governmental structure in isolation, but by the government as it exists and is understood in a political and societal context.

The addition of communication technology can be seen simply as an increase in efficiency, but in reshaping the resources required to participate or transmit ideas the functions of the state can, and will, change, often in unintended ways. In seeing change engineered as a complex interaction of social factors, the focus on a single event or mistake has limited explanatory power (Hadari 1989; Schickler 2001). Power is often in the unintended consequences, instead of the goals of actors and institutions. Significant political theorists such as Adam Smith, Georg Hegel, and Jean-Paul Sartre have considered the impact of the unintended interplay of social forces as pivotal (Hegel and Kaufmann 1977; Sartre 1976; Smith 1991).

While there are many technological innovations that can influence the nature and structure of the American political system, the revolution in communication technology is likely the most significant. Understanding the scope and degree of this change is difficult, as the technology has been assimilated slowly and often with little or no immediate change. Nonetheless, there is little argument that advancing communication technology is changing the nature of the political landscape (Allison 2002; Klotz 2004; Saco 2002; Shapiro 1999; Wilhelm 2000). By integrating technology into the functions of government, we have altered, in fundamental ways, the power dynamics of our political system. Though most notable in electoral forums, technology growth is affecting the way that government goes about its tasks in almost every aspect. From filing taxes to obtaining federal documents, the manner by which the government interacts with the people is changing rapidly.

As noted above, one of the most difficult aspects of measuring a stimulus such as technology is effectively recognizing a change produced by a unique convergence of ideas, institutional structure, and the stimulus itself. We have theorized that the growth of communication technology as exemplified by the Internet will change the nature of the political structure in the United States. It is possible that the most significant impact of the Internet is an indirect consequence of its use in voting. The most noteworthy impact of the Internet may be as part of the electoral machinery itself. This is not a projected or theoretical assertion about the possible use of the Internet. E-voting, or remote voting over the Internet, is no longer fiction. In actual practice, e-voting allows people with Internet access to avoid going to the physical location of the polls and vote online for candidates or ballot issues. This can be accomplished at home or from work, or at any location with an Internet connection. With the increase of wireless Internet options, also known as hot spots, the locations are growing for e-voting as long as the voter has access to a computer with the requisite technology. In the private sector, companies such as Chevron and Lucent Technologies have utilized e-voting as a means to elect union officers (Nathan 2000). Universities such as Stanford and the University of

Florida have used it for student government elections. States such as Iowa and Washington have experimented with Internet ballots.

The largest breakthrough in e-voting originated with the Arizona Democratic Party, which initiated an entirely new political discourse by allowing its members to vote over the Internet in the 2000 Democratic presidential primary. Shortly after the election, an early survey conducted by faculty at Arizona State suggested some possible impacts of the Internet voting. Arizona had a sharp rise in electoral participation, with the turnout increasing 723 percent from 1996 to 2000 (Solop 2001). Solop noted the demographic impact of the election primarily with regard to age, education, and religion (Solop 2001). Though empirically interesting, the early work did not attempt to create a theoretical framework for exploring the possibly significant change in the voting population should e-voting be adopted in other jurisdictions. We create such a framework and test it empirically. The proposition herein is that the Internet may crystallize a substantial technological gap in the voting electorate that could exacerbate cleavages already present within the electorate. More generally, the Internet very well may change the magnitude of previously existing voter turnout cleavages based on income, race, and age, and thereby force a substantial change in how politicians campaign and govern. Though the scope of a single primary is in itself too small to make sweeping generalities about the national electorate, it should supply indicators of the potential exacerbation of preexisting cleavages in the electorate.

COST OF VOTING AND THE INTERNET

To understand the impact of the technology of e-voting on the electoral system, an analytic framework must be created to judge the effect of the technology. E-voting presents a new and potentially significant variable in the analysis of voting behavior, but it does not change the fundamental structure of such analysis. Voting and the political system are unchanged, but the use of the Internet changes the means and operation of the system at a fundamental level by adding a new procedural lens to the equation. From a social choice perspective, e-voting does not change the calculus of voting as developed by Downs (1957) and later adopted with a slightly different emphasis by Riker and Ordeshook (Barry 1978; Riker and Ordeshook 1968; Tullock 1967). The gravamen of this understanding of the reasons for voting is based in economic principles as understood by behavioralist political scientists. The basic premise is that people will vote when the benefit to them outweighs the cost of voting. This is expressed by Downs in a slightly more refined equation as follows:

$$R = PB - C$$

In the equation, the R denotes the net reward or utility in voting, or more simply the net benefit. The likelihood of voting is a function of the probability that the vote will affect the outcome P multiplied by the differential benefit of the voter's candidate B prevailing and then subtracting the cost of voting C. The C represents the cost of voting, which would include the length of the wait or the difficulty in traveling to the polls or even the time, energy, or money required to become educated about candidates and issues. Understood in purely mathematical terms, the theory contends that the voter will abstain from voting if $R < 0$. Also note that if $R > 0$, the voter still may abstain because there may be other competing activities that produce a higher R for that given point in time.

The formula makes several assumptions. Assuming that the cost $C > 0$, then PB must be $> C$ for the voter to vote. As noted in several reviews of the calculus of voting, the probability that any particular vote will affect the outcome almost always is going to be very small and approach zero, which will require that the potential benefit or B must be very large for a vote to occur (Blais 2000; Gill and Gainous 2002). Obviously, it would take an unrealistically large value for B to overcome this small value of P. Riker and Ordeshook (1968) attempt to account for this problem by formalizing the additional Downsian satisfaction parameter D. This D is added to the equation and represents the personal satisfaction/utility that a citizen receives from the act of voting regardless of the actual outcome of the election. The revised equation is as follows:

$$R = PB + D - C$$

Where the cost to vote C outweighs the potential utility to affect the outcome and the perceived benefit plus the various sub-factors mentioned above, the voter is not likely to vote. The equation represents the base decision-making of a voter grounded on a basic notion of utility maximization with the inclusion of the less quantifiable variable of duty D, which acts largely as an error or stochastic term. As becomes readily apparent, anything that affects

any of the variables in the equation can change the nature of the voting electorate. As a mathematical formula, the calculus of voting lacks a universality
that most economists and mathematicians would prefer. Part of the problem
is the inability to measure personal satisfaction, which would appear to vary
not just across demographics, but also across individuals living in the same
household. Riker and Ordeshook (1968) contend that this D value is not
constant across individuals. Therefore, some will vote and some will abstain,
depending on whether Di sufficiently overcomes Ci for individual i. D is said
to consist of various social and psychological subfactors such as: citizen duty,
prestige, guilt relief, and a sense of continuing the political system (Blais
2000). Nonetheless, the more basic premise, when understood in a more
conceptual understanding, still is useful.

In using the Downsian construct, we are not contending that this quantita-
tive formulation of voting based on rational or social choice principles is the
only way to measure or predict voter turnout. Indeed, the model suffers from
the limitations observed about most social choice constructs, which depend
too much on economic motives and avoid societal or social context and
structure (Blais 2000; Green and Shapiro 1996). Nonetheless, it does provide
a logical framework in which to understand how the Internet can affect voting
patterns. While the positive component of the model is a function of several
factors, the central drag on participation is just one variable: cost of voting
(C). Downs (1957) refers to this component as the opportunity cost of voting based on the time and resources spent in preparing for, and participating
in, the election. More recently, this cost has been more succinctly described
as the cost of registration, decision making, and turnout at the polls (Aldrich
1995). Though each of these elements is a valid cost associated with participation, the cost of physically turning out at the polls seems to be the most significant. Research on the National Voter Registration Act (Motor Voter) has
illustrated that reduced registration cost alone appears insufficient to bring
voters to the polls (Martinez and Hill 1999).

The initial question presented herein is what would happen if technology
shifted some of the basic cost of voting away from a demographic or demographics of people? More succinctly, could one change voter participation
by simply changing the nature of the most substantive elements in the cost
of voting? By voting on the Internet from home and eliminating entirely the
cost of turning out at the polls, the drag on participation should significantly

decline. Further, it follows that those who vote on the Internet also would benefit from the information-gathering ability offered by the Internet, enabling them to reduce the resources spent in preparing to vote and in learning about the candidates and their issues (Browning 2002; Davis 1999). As a result, the Internet should significantly reduce the magnitude of the drag variable in the equation. As noted above, registration cost alone does not appear to be a significant drag on turnout, though this issue is unsettled (Martinez and Hill 1999; Wolfinger and Rosenstone 1980). Nonetheless, the Internet also may be used to reduce the cost of registration as well. In Arizona, the voters in the primary were contacted through mail with Internet voting instructions (Solop 2001). In the future, much of the registration could be performed with little or no cost online.

The implications of this change should be substantial. If the cost of voting C is reduced, turnout should change. Turnout, if measured in magnitude alone, is interesting, and as mentioned above, previous work has illustrated that turnout did substantially increase in Arizona during the Internet primary. But such a finding is not the end of the analysis. The more significant issue is based not on magnitude of turnout, but in the possible change within the voting electorate itself. More directly, the issue is whether the Internet changes the identity of the voter at the poll or the likelihood of different groups voting. Generally, the Internet should lower in absolute terms the true cost of voting in the voting equation, but it is not uniform in its application. The ability to use the Internet is based on the availability of a computer connected to the Internet combined with sufficient knowledge of its use. One only gets the benefit of a reduced cost of voting when these threshold factors are met. Without access and knowledge, the cost of voting equation remains unchanged. Hence, the benefit and impact of the Internet is built on a divided foundation of haves and have-nots (Davis 1999). The Internet will not disenfranchise anyone, but rather will disadvantage non-users as voting participants (Davis 1999).

VOTING AND THE DIGITAL DIVIDE: MAXIMIZING THE INEQUALITY EFFECT

Historically, the patterns of participation in the United States have not been based on equity. In *Luther v. Borden* (1849), the United States Supreme Court upheld the right of states to limit the electorate to only freeholders, as the original charter in Rhode Island did. While the court has moved toward granting access to the polls as is evidenced by the voting rights cases, even the increase in access to voting has failed to create a voting system that provides equivalent turnout among demographic groups. Under the present voting system, the United States has managed to combine declining turnout with increasingly unbalanced voting electorates that over-represent the upper classes (Burnham 1987; Leighley and Nagler 1992; Rosenstone and Hansen 1993). We propose that the use of e-voting will not only be consistent with this trend, but will, with increasing impact, crystallize the distinction by changing the voting incentive and costs in the voting system along an increasingly apparent cleavage. The end result will not be a question of over-representation, but rather of significant power growth in favored groups. Where Motor Voter was expected to help balance the electorate through increased registration of under-represented groups (Martinez and Hill 1999), e-voting will emphasize a technological and class gap through the more significant reduction of the turnout cost in these favored groups.

There are significant sociological divisions in both the access and use of the Internet for Americans based on income, race, and age. These divisions are strikingly similar to the types of divisions that already exist in our electoral system that over-represents those of higher socioeconomic status. Figure 4.1 traces the percent of Americans that use the Internet based on whether they are above or below the median income in the nation. From 2000 to 2008, upper-income Americans' use rate hovers around 80 percent while the lower-income Americans stay mostly near or just above 40 percent. Lower-income Americans will lack not only the access to computers in the home, but also the training and experience to use them for multiple purposes, including voting, should that become an option.

Similarly, there are significant variations in the use of the Internet among different racial categories in the United States. As seen in figure 4.2, African Americans substantially trail both Caucasians and Latinos in the use of the Internet. While figure 4.2 shows gains across all groups in Internet use, African Americans continue to trail by at least 10 percent from 2000 through 2008. The divisions across racial lines are important in the context of voting as race is an important factor in both participation and partisan politics. Voting on the Internet may well exacerbate some of the participation cleavages that are already seen among different racial groups if the differences in usage do not narrow.

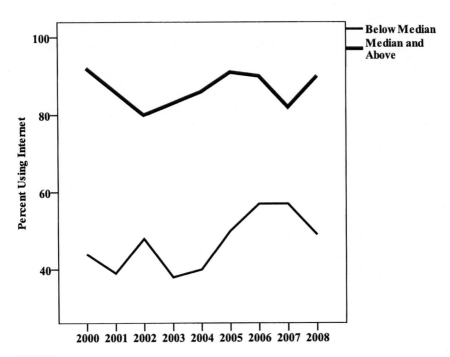

FIGURE 4.1
The Income Divide across Time

Source: Pew Internet & American Life Project 2000–2008. The first released data from each year containing
the necessary indicators were selected.

Finally, there are important participation issues associated with age. In
the United States older voters turn out in higher numbers in most national
elections (Rosenstone and Hansen 1993). Yet, this is one area that voting on
the Internet may well favor the lower participation group. Figure 4.3 shows
Internet use divided between those thirty-five and under compared to those
over thirty-five. As expected, the younger cohort uses the Internet at a higher
rate, though the gap seems to be narrowing. In March 2000, about 78 percent
of the younger cohort was using the Internet with only 50 percent of the older
cohort online. By 2008, slightly more than 80 percent of the younger cohort
was using the Internet compared to 65 percent of the older cohort. The difference between the two cohorts had narrowed by almost half.

Some of these distinctions might be less relevant considering that Internet
voting can occur outside the home at places of public access. Internet access
is available for people through schools and libraries. Yet, for the purpose of

FIGURE 4.2
The Racial Divide across Time

Source: Pew Internet & American Life Project 2000–2008. The first released data from each year containing
the necessary indicators were selected.

the cost of voting analysis, there is no significant difference between traveling to the local polling location versus the local library. Further, only a small
fraction of Americans use computers at community centers (Department of
Commerce 2000). Hence, the cost of voting reduction is largely through remote access. Conceivably, however, the analysis may change should Internet
voting be made more widely and readily available through remote units than
traditional polling stations. If the data are consistent with the utility model,
there should be an observable movement in favor of groups with technology.
Based on divisions identified by the data from the United States Department of Commerce on access and use of technology, the results from the
Arizona primary based on the cost benefit of the Internet should be reflected

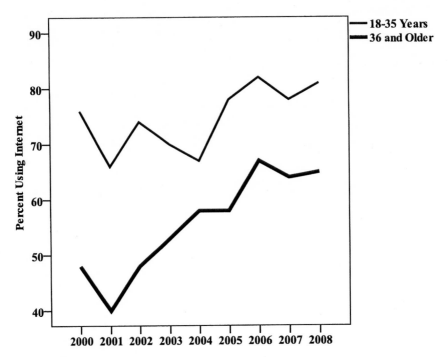

FIGURE 4.3
The Age Divide across Time

Source: Pew Internet & American Life Project 2000–2008. The first released data from each year containing the necessary indictors were selected.

in economic, racial, and age demographics. Aware of criticism based on the digital divide, Arizona did provide Internet voting through computer polling stations (Solop 2001). As this does not provide any substantial cost benefit related to turnout, this analysis is focused solely on the remote Internet voting data.

Ultimately, we are theorizing that e-voting will magnify the advantages of certain demographic groups in the electorate. This is significant, since it changes who will get elected, what groups will influence the selection process, and ultimately what policies will be enacted. What makes this particularly noteworthy is that this is an inadvertent result of technology. Scholars have observed some long-term changes that result from short-term adaptations, though these are often the result of individual choices made over extended periods of time rather than systematic changes in the larger system (Schickler 2001). In the case of technology, the implications are often difficult to anticipate, as the ramifications are often peripheral to the intended effect. It is true that electoral systems often are deliberately designed to produce a certain result (Riker 1986), as in the case of our original institutional design. Nonetheless, e-voting is not expressly intended to change the balance of the electoral system. E-voting simply is a variable added to a constitutional construct designed centuries ago with no understanding of the improvements in communication technology or the changes in the greater society that would occur to favor more direct expressions of public will. This is a direct result of technology providing the stimuli for change and society ultimately adjusting and shifting in response.

As noted above, the theory of electoral change proposed herein is but one facet of the stimulus generated by the shifting communication technology as evidenced by the growing popularity of the Internet. Nonetheless, it is a significant one with very little notice being ascribed to the power of voting technology to impact and shift voting results. Most of the scholarship associated with the Internet continues to focus on the issue of security, which clearly is significant. The importance of voting security has slowed the adoption of e-voting, with no states using the process in light of the controversies surrounding the presidential election of 2000 and the complaints about touchscreen voting in the subsequent presidential election of 2004.

DATA

Our model tests the probable impact of certain demographic characteristics on Internet voting. The model and methods are described below. First, we specify the measurement of the dependent and independent variables. As noted in chapter 2, the dependent variable is remote Internet turnout and is measured as a percentage of the total turnout by county.

As for independent variables, income per capita was measured using the Census Bureau data by individual unit of population, or by county. The mean income per capita of all counties is $16,942. Income was divided by 1000 to make the interpretation of the output more intuitive. In our data, income and education are correlated closely, making the inclusion of both variables redundant (r = 0.69, p < 0.01). To make each individual case (county) relative to every other respective case, the demographic indicators of race and age were converted to percentages by county. White, African American, and

Latino were all conformed to percentages using the following simple formula: Total Population by Race per County/Total Population per County. These percentages were then multiplied by 100 to make the interpretation more intuitive. The mean percentage of whites by county was 0.70, African Americans by county was 0.02, and Latinos by county was 0.27. The Native American population, which is significant in Arizona, was not included in the model to create a baseline variable.

The percentage of adolescents was measured and inferred based on a raw number of persons under eighteen with a mean of 91,130 and a median of 33,425 converted with the same formula: (Total Population by Age per County/Total Population per County) $\times$ 100. This variable is intended to measure the proportional presence of families which serves as an indicator of young and middle-aged potential voters who are more likely to use the Internet to vote as the theory herein contends. Population over sixty-five was also measured as a ratio using the same formula as above. Senior citizens had a mean and median of 0.15 and 0.14, respectively. These averages do not differ much from the national average, except perhaps for the lower percentage of African Americans and higher percentage of Latinos (Department of Commerce 2000). This does not threaten the generalizability of our model because it is primarily an argument of socioeconomic class structure that is associated with race. The combination of African Americans with Latinos in Arizona approaches the combination of their national averages (Department of Commerce 2000).

METHODS

The Bayesian Way

The small sample size makes conventional Null Hypotheses Significance Tests (NHST) problematic. This concern is addressed by the use of a Bayesian construct which involves the creation of posterior subjective probability distributions of model parameters by combining prior information (non-sample knowledge) with sample data (Gill 2002; Western and Jackman 1994). Using a small N sample has become less controversial. Bayesian methods have been advocated for research involving a small number of observations and cases involving non-stochastic data. Small datasets that produce fragile statistical inference in frequentist models are more effectively handled by the Bayesian approach through the incorporation of prior information in the estimation. This methodology provides a solution to problems associated with restricted samples and collinearity (Robert 2001). In a previous study, Western and Jackman (1994) use Bayesian inferential methods with a sample size of twenty.

As noted above, the Bayesian process of data analysis allows researchers to incorporate previous knowledge into a statistical model. This is operationalized through prior distributions, which are descriptions of relative probabilities that are usually based on previous research and knowledge developed in the discipline (Gill 2002). In order to create our Bayesian model we included a prior distribution for each of our variables based on the findings of the Solop (2001) study. These prior distributions are described in greater detail below.

Aside from dealing with the limitations of conventional NHST models, the Bayesian approach also allows us to make probability statements about the parameters of the model. The outcome is not a point estimate as in an NHST model, but rather a probability distribution that is typically described by a mean or mode and some type of measurement of dispersion (Jackman 2000). In contrast to the NHST method of deciding strength of conclusions based on the magnitude of p-values, Bayesian inference presents evidence by simply summarizing the posterior distribution, and therefore there is no artificial decision based on the assumption of a true null hypothesis. Posterior summary is typically done with quantiles and probability statements, such as the probability that the parameter of interest is less than/greater than some interesting constant, or the probability that this parameter occupies some region. While a brief discussion and review of the Bayesian approach is undertaken in this chapter, a complete review of the applicability of Bayesian methodology is beyond the scope of this book (for a complete review see Gill 2002; Robert 2001; Pollard 1986; Lee 1989; Western and Jackman 1994).

Modeling Remote Internet Turnout

Though Bayesian inference permits a wide range of modeling specifications, the design used for this study is based on a standard ordinary least squares (OLS) regression that is supplemented by the prior information provided in the Solop study. None of the Gauss-Markov assumptions are violated, and therefore, ordinary least-squares regression is the best linear unbiased estimator of the relationship. The association between the

outcome variable percent remote Internet turnout by county and the explanatory variables is linear, and is modeled as follows before integrating
prior information:

$$Y = \alpha + \beta \text{ income} + \beta \text{ percent black} + \beta \text{ percent white} + \beta \text{ percent Latino}$$
$$+ \beta \text{ percent over 65} + \beta \text{ percent adolescent} + e$$

Inclusion of Prior Information

Our non-sample information used for the creation of the Bayesian prior
is drawn from previous research on the Arizona primary (Solop 2001). These
data include three telephone surveys: a 1,200-person cross-sectional survey
of Arizona adults, a 1,200-person survey of registered Democrats in Arizona,
and a post-election panel study with 783 registered Democrats, of which 318
participated in the Democratic primary (Solop 2001). The prior distributions
on the explanatory variables are all based on a normal distribution, with the
mean centered on the prior information derived from the Solop (2001) study.
The mean of each of the relevant Solop variables is adopted as the mean of
the prior distributions. Since our prior is based upon a single survey instrument instead of a compilation of research, we operationalize our uncertainty
through the variance placed on the prior distributions. Larger variances
reflect greater uncertainty. The variance is operationalized by what is called
the prior precision. The precision is inversely related to variance, hence,
lower precision provides for greater variance. The precision on the variables
measuring income, race, and age are set at 0.0001 to create a largely diffuse
prior, so as to indicate relative uncertainty in the model. As there is only one
inferential study of the impact of Internet voting, using a tight or well-defined
prior would presume a state of knowledge that is not representative of the
current level of scholarship.[1]

Based on the Solop study of Internet voting, the means of our prior distributions representing the rate of participation in the Internet primary were set
from the statistical results reported in the referenced study as follows: percent
white (0.47), percent Latino (0.44), and percent over 65 (0.33). These values
represent the percentage of Internet voting derived from the Solop survey. Solop factored income into several categories, and we selected the mean Internet
turnout expected by his highest category (≥ $75K), setting the mean to 0.69.
Two of the variables used in the model (percent black and percent adolescent)

were not measured in previous studies so we supply a diffuse normal prior with a mean at zero to indicate the lack of information for these variables.

The data from the Solop study provide an important foundation for our own data, which are based on a county-level aggregate sample. The limited sample size would prevent us from reaching the commonly accepted threshold for statistical inference in a frequentist model (Western and Jackman 1994). But the combination of the prior information with the present sample allows for asymptotic inference. The data provide the base parameters for the prior distribution of the explanatory variables.

Obtaining the Posterior through Simulation

To create the distribution of the posterior for the parameters of interest, we used Gibbs's sampling method of Markov Chain Monte Carlo (MCMC). The Gibbs sampler integrates the posterior identity to create probability inferences for each of the unknown parameters in the model. The underlying premise of this technique is that if an iterative chain of consecutive values can be set up carefully and run long enough, then empirical estimations of quantities of interest can be obtained from chain values. In order to estimate multidimensional probability structures such as our posterior distributions, we began a Markov Chain in the sample space and let it run until it settled into the correct distribution. From this distribution we were able to gather statistics including the means, variances, and quantiles from the simulated posterior.

The model was operationalized through the use of WinBugs, a program for Bayesian analysis of complex statistical models using MCMC techniques. The Bayesian approach is direct and open with all of the assumptions delineated in the equation itself. As indicated above, the outcome variable is assumed to be distributed normally around the systematic component with fixed variance. The systematic effect is based on a linear specification but includes a random effects term. The hyper-parameter is based on a tightly defined gamma distribution for the precision in this variable, allowing for a random effects model. The gamma distribution is appropriate because it is the conjugate of the normal distribution, and our likelihood function utilizes the normal distribution. Instead of having a constant precision, the model will draw on the gamma distribution for that parameter. All of the coefficient estimates are given diffuse normal priors but are centered on information obtained from the Solop surveys.

FINDINGS

The results of our Bayesian inference are presented in table 4.1. The table describes the posterior distributions of the variables in our model. While frequentist models provide point references, Bayesian output is the description of probability distributions rather than a single point. The distributions can be described by their means and standard deviation. The mean is the tangent of the distribution, or the most likely effect of the explanatory variable on the outcome variable. The credible interval describes the bounds of the distributional effects of the explanatory variables that serve as predictors of e-voting based on our sample and non-sample (prior) information. For the purpose of this paper, we have used a 95% credible interval. Significance can be interpreted negatively or positively from a credible interval bounded away from zero in either direction.

The posterior distributions in the instant model offer sufficient evidence to provide support to the theory that Internet voting lowers the costs of voting for certain demographic groups. There is a positive relationship between income and remote Internet turnout, a negative relationship between age and remote Internet turnout, and a negative relationship between the Latino population and remote Internet turnout. While there is some conflicting evidence in the results regarding race because of the positive relationship between the black population and remote Internet turnout, these discrepancies can be accounted for by the fact that the data are at the aggregate level. This assertion is further explored in the interpretation of each of the explanatory effects explained by the model.

Though not large in absolute terms, as income increases, remote Internet voting increases when controlling for the other demographic variables. Zero is not bounded in the 95% credible interval (0.44 to 1.36) and the mean effect is 0.90. This indicates that the true unknown parameter while controlling for the other demographic indicators within the model is positive around approximately 95 percent of the time. This finding contradicts that of the Solop (2001) study, wherein his binary logistical regression indicated that income was not significant. This is noteworthy as our results differ from the previous study concerning the effect of income despite incorporating the earlier work into the Bayesian prior. Nonetheless, this result is consistent with what one would expect from one of the major indicators of growing class division.

The model is consistent with the expected relationship between race and remote Internet turnout. As can be seen in table 4.1, there is a negative relationship between Latino voters and remote Internet turnout while holding all other explanatory variables constant. The 95% credible interval indicates that this negative relationship between Latino voters and remote Internet turnout is reliable (-25.61 to -11.04). The expected relationship also exists for white voters. The distribution indicates a positive relationship with a 95% credible interval bounded away from zero (17.4 to 41.83). The distribution is well defined and the mean of the distribution is reliably positive.

The test results of the relationship between the African American population and remote Internet turnout are not what we expected. The relationship appears to be positive with the mean well above zero at 105.6. This may be based upon the demographic makeup of Arizona. The African American population in Arizona is relatively small and the variance between each county is extremely low. Therefore, there is not enough change in the explanatory value, case by case, to produce a significant change in the outcome variable. In addition, the highest of the African American populations are in urban areas that also have high income ($r = 0.65$, $p < 0.01$), so the variance is absorbed by the income explanatory variable in the opposite direction of what would be expected from low-income families. It is simply a product of aggregate categories.

Age is consistently viewed as having predictive value for Internet and computer use and that view is supported by the most recent census indicating

Table 4.1. Explanatory Posterior Distributions of Internet Voting

	Mean Effects	S. D.	95% Credible Intervals	
Income	0.90	0.23	0.44	1.36
Percent Black	105.60	39.97	25.88	183.40
Percent White	29.65	6.22	17.40	41.83
Percent Latino	−18.35	3.69	−25.61	−11.04
Percent Over 65	−66.34	14.79	−95.37	−36.98
Percent Adolescent	39.91	8.10	24.45	56.23
Constant	0.92	2.21	3.57	3.90
Posterior Standard Error	0.90			
Number of Cases	15			

Note: Data were obtained from the Arizona Democratic Party and the U.S. Census 2000.

that homes headed by persons under fifty are more likely to own a computer (DOC 2000). Our model is consistent with these indicators and shows a strong negative relationship between age and Internet voting. For persons over sixty-five the negative relationship with Internet voting is apparent. The credible interval is negative and bounded away from zero illustrating 95% probability that the true unknown parameter of age influence on remote Internet turnout is between -95.37 and -36.98. This illustrates that age is a powerful predictor of Internet use and voting. The distribution is centered far from zero at -66.34.

The credible interval generated by the measure of adolescence further exhibits the strong negative relationship of age to e-voting (24.45 and 56.23). While the distribution of this variable indicates a positive relationship, the true nature of the relationship to age is inverted because the variable is measured as a percentage of youth. As the presence of adolescents increases, so does the presence of parents who are generally younger than sixty-five. Hence, as age decreases, e-voting increases. This posterior distribution has a mean and standard deviation of 39.91 and 8.10 respectively. The age indicators can also be thought of as a propensity for the use of technology. In the present context, there is a strong gap between younger families with technology and the older populations who are lagging behind in the increasingly complex digital age (DOC 2000). The younger generation is likely to have fewer problems with technology-driven advances. County-level aggregate data do not allow for a more detailed view of the youth effect, though the greater penetration of technology to younger Americans is worth further study. It is unclear from these data that age will be a constant division. It may be that some of the age-related divisions are not so much a matter of life cycle, but are founded on generational differences that will decline over time as the more technically savvy generations reach retirement.

Diagnostics

The reliability of a posterior generated through MCMC is based upon an assumption of convergence. More succinctly, the posterior described must come after the Markov chains have found the regions of highest density in the sample space for each indicator. MCMC samplers will usually get to a desired distribution, though it may take many iterations to achieve convergence. There is no perfect way to make this determination, though there are several different tests of convergence. We used the widely accepted Gelman and Rubin (1992) convergence diagnostic. This procedure measures the within-chain variance and between-chain variance for multiple chains with diffuse starting points. A score of 1.2 or less is considered acceptable. In testing our model, all of the relevant posteriors achieved a Gelman and Rubin score of near 1.0. We also confirmed convergence using the Geweke (1993) test, as well as by performing a visual inspection of the chains through the use of trace plots.[2]

MODERN E-VOTING

Arizona's Democratic primary was the first use of the Internet in an actual political election in the United States, but it was not the only use. The Republican Party also experimented with a straw poll in 2000 in Alaska. This was a small-scale process with an estimated 3,500 Republicans expected to cast their ballots by computer (Browder 2006). Alaska seems a particularly appropriate venue as it has remote rural districts. Alaskan voters would have an easier time voting from a computer than journeying to polling stations. Yet, there was little evidence that Alaskan voters were ready for Internet voting in 2000 (Gallen 2005). Only thirty-five Alaskans cast their ballots online (Barr 2005). Certainly part of the difficulty was the lack of Internet infrastructure in Alaska in 2000, especially the light penetration of broadband services such as DSL into the rural areas. Even with Bayesian methods, the number of Internet voters in Alaska is far too small to draw any conclusions about the likely implications of e-voting on the composition of the electorate.

Internet voting was also used in the Michigan Democratic primary of 2004, though only as an option for voters who had already requested an absentee ballot through traditional methods. In the case of Michigan, there is little evidence of any electoral bias, though this finding is limited by the restricted nature of the Michigan process (Prevost and Schaffner 2008). If there was any bias in the Michigan election, it was a procedural one. Internet voting was only possible if the voter had the foresight to request an absentee ballot weeks ahead of the election. As a result, there was little cost benefit to the procedure for the average voter. For our purposes, the Arizona primary remains the better indicator of likely Internet implications as it was not as structurally confined.

The best examples of Internet voting are outside the United States. While international experiences are largely beyond the scope of this book, the Estonian voting procedures are noteworthy. Like the United States, several

European nations, including France, the Netherlands, Switzerland, and the United Kingdom, have tried some version of Internet voting even if just a limited trial or experiment (Alvarez, Hall, and Trechsel 2009). However, no nation has implemented Internet voting to the extent of the former Soviet Republic of Estonia. Beginning in 2005, when American states were still considering or experimenting with Internet voting, Estonia conducted two nationwide elections in which all voters were eligible to vote online. The number of Internet voters as a percentage of the electorate was relatively small, but it is growing. In 2005, 1.9 percent of voters used the Internet to vote. The percentage increased to 5.4 percent in 2007 (Alvarez, Hall, and Trechsel 2009).

Estonia's experience presents a window into some of the digital divide issues discussed in this chapter. Studies of the Estonian Internet voting show that Internet voting favors younger voters and voters with experience in computers and technology. However, there is no evidence of race or gender divides, though the ethnic Russian population has had trouble voting online (Alvarez, Hall, and Trechsel 2009). In that sense, Estonia is a mixed verdict on the digital divide. Estonia's population is more homogeneous than the United States,' its population is generally well educated, and the Internet penetration is significant across the nation. As a result, it is hard to argue that the absence of race or gender issues, or other divisions in Estonia, necessarily projects to the American electorate where sociological divisions such as race are far more significant and long standing. However, it is a signal that in the right circumstances the Internet can be implemented in a relatively neutral fashion.

CONCLUSION

The data and findings herein are but a preliminary look at what likely will be a growing field related to the impact of the Internet on voting and behavior. As e-voting becomes more prevalent, more samples will become available to test rational voting models and the cleavages suggested herein. The research herein is being used to suggest a rational utility model as a means to view the impact of the Internet on the voting electorate. Though this certainly is not the only impact, the declining cost of voting may, by maximizing the voting strength of certain groups, reshape voting trends and call for a new calculus in creating likely voter models. Though the data suggest that there will be no sharp change in who votes, it does indicate a magnification of the economic cleavage that already has been observed. The effect of an acceleration of this shift can be explored in multiple policy areas and in the decline in power of some demographic groups. Further, some of the change may well be new. If the trend continues to show a small over-sixty-five presence on the net combined with growing youth usage, the power dynamic of interest groups such as the American Association of Retired Persons could change.

But ultimately, the nature of the Internet and its future relationship to voting behavior is unsettled. In chapter 3, we explored some of the elements of the digital divide. Age and education continue to be significant variables and the issue of race is still significant for multiple ethnicities in the United States, including the growing population of Latinos, as illustrated in table 3.4. Age and socioeconomic status are important predictors of online political use. Though these might vary or change with time, they do exist and will for some time into the future.

As noted earlier, the availability as well as use of the technology is changing, and thus, the cost of voting model is not static with relation to the electorate. The import of the above findings was not to prove that e-voting will be the most significant development in the growth of communications technology, or even that the findings above are a complete representation of the future. Indeed, they cannot be. In the end, with larger efforts to distribute technology and with the growth of homes with Internet access, there may well be some equity in the impact of the Internet across demographic barriers and groups. The Internet has become an integral part of American society. According to a Pew Survey, the Internet has grown into a major form of communication. In 1993, only 3 percent of Americans used the Internet. By 2003, 67 percent of Americans have claimed to have at some time been online (Klotz 2004). Our own measures in chapter 2 show the trend toward greater access. While this is short of having a computer in every home, the expansive growth of the Internet in society is remarkable for its speed and penetration in areas ranging from the home, to the office, to public facilities such as libraries and schools (Klotz 2004). Yet, it is just as clear that at present, there is a sharp contrast in the initial benefit of the technology. In the infancy of e-voting, this may have a significant impact on how campaigns are managed and how voters impact the government.

Bowling Online

The Internet and the New Social Capital

Robert Putnam (1995a, 1995b, 2000) makes the sweeping claim that decaying social capital, or the interconnectedness between people, is causing a decline in political participation. Further, that as a result the viability of democracy is threatened. While many have challenged this premise (Althaus 1998; Arneil 2006; McDonald and Popkin 2001; Portes 1998), we offer a different perspective. Rather, we suggest that the Internet is shaping a new kind of political participation and engagement. It is creating networks and interactivity on scales that are larger in scope and implication than at any time in American history. Thus, we present an alternative view of the American political future that is substantively different from the theories of declining participation and lower rates of belief in the system that have dominated the scholarship within political behavior. Concurring with Putnam, we also suggest that democracy is rooted in an understanding of social networks and communicated ideas but believe that, potentially, the Internet is a solution to decaying social capital and the decline of political participation. Using advances such as Web 2.0, it promotes social capital through networking with a speed, interactivity, and versatility that were never before possible. While the ultimate implications of this modern Internet society are and will be unclear for some time, the initial data suggest that there is a far more rich and diverse engagement of people with government than political scientists have been willing to concede.

Specifically, the findings presented in this chapter suggest several things. First, building on the results presented in chapter 2, people are networking on the Internet in a variety of different ways including social network sites, e-mail, and blogs. Second, the degree to which people are doing so varies across the same types of demographics and behavioral indicators that predicted the degree to which people use the Internet to gather information (see chapter 3). This variation is fairly consistent across the Pew Data and Student Data. Third, and most central to the premise here, heightened social networking on the Internet is positively related to political participation, both voting and broadly defined, in the Pew and Student Data even when controlling for traditional predictors of such. Finally, for exploratory purposes, we look at the possibility that social networking could actually be related to vote choice. Interestingly, we find that among the typically young respondents in the Student Data, those who do more networking on the Internet are more likely to vote for Democrats. Before moving on to the analysis, we present a theory as to the likely impact of the Internet on participation and discuss the literature that has explored similar questions.

RETHINKING THE PARTICIPATION PUZZLE

Within this literature, perhaps the most widely disseminated and durable explanation of the continued viability of democratic government and its more recent decline is Robert Putnam's (1995a, 1995b, 2000) theory of social capital. Putnam contends that democracies are dependent on social capital, or social connections that generate trust. "Social capital" is defined as the "norms of reciprocity and networks of civil engagement" which are created by participation in groups such as civil organizations (1995a: 167). People, engaging with each other though social and civic groups, create bonds tying and investing them into the greater society. It also works well in providing the mechanism for the transmission of information along the lines theorized by Page and Shapiro (1992) and Popkin (1991). Isolated people cannot share experiences and make informed aggregate decisions. Nor are they able to develop working heuristic shortcuts.

Some have suggested that the Internet may stimulate participation by increasing voter information (Tolbert and McNeal 2003). Social networking via the Internet may be the impetus for increasing voter information. Returning to the original puzzle, social capital has become a popular lens to use in describing the perceived decline in turnout and participation in the U.S. electoral system. Various measures have been used to illustrate that the United States has managed to combine declining turnout with increasingly unbalanced voting electorates that over-represent the upper classes (Burnham 1987; Leighley and Nagler 1992; Rosenstone and Hansen 1993). These observations dovetail with Putnam's explanation that the decline of social capital, as measured in large part through decreasing participation in civic groups and civic activities, is leading to fewer voters and a less viable democracy. Putnam presents many factors that may or may not be hurting social capital, but he saves particular emphasis for the negative role of television which correlates with anti-civic behavior. The underlying proposition is that only through the revival of civic groups, such as the once-popular bowling league, can the foundations of American democracy be stabilized (Putnam 1995b, 2000).

Before addressing Putnam's chief assumptions, it is noteworthy that while the decline thesis has been dominant within the literature, it is not unchallenged. There is some suggestion that both the perceived lack of information and the progressively lesser turnout are produced by poor measures rather than true representations of trends (Althaus 1998; McDonald and Popkin 2001; Achen 1975). Nonetheless, it is beyond the scope of this book to again take up the methodological debate. We attack the underlying theoretical premise itself. The major problem with the decline thesis itself is that it presumes a fairly static environment and an unchanging greater society.

Presuming for a moment that Putnam has correctly identified that shared interaction and engagement is foundational for democracy, his static view of human interaction leads to a faulty prescription. How people interact and engage with each other is not the same today as it was immediately after World War II. In searching for evidence of these phenomena, Putnam seeks out measures based on civic institutions that are either no longer extant or are in serious decline, leading him to predict a less optimistic democratic future. We suggest that any measure of civic engagement that relies on an analysis of the means of interaction is flawed. For example, a measure of social interaction could be done by counting the number of conversations an individual has with different people within a day. If one were to measure these conversations by face-to-face communication the trend would be stark. After the invention and dissemination of the telephone, the measure would surely show decline, even if in reality, people were speaking to each other with greater frequency by means of telecommunication.

CHALLENGING THE DECLINE THESIS

The difficulty with assessing any theory of participation is in making sure that what is measured is a fair representation of how people engage each other during a fixed temporal period. Yet, nothing remains fixed over time. Technology growth is affecting the way that government goes about its tasks in almost every aspect. While there is little argument that the Internet has changed the nature of political campaigning, it often is difficult to measure this change. Thus, the impact often is addressed more speculatively rather than with empirical data.[1]

If one is to take issue with Robert Putnam's prevalent theory that a disconnected society is causing a decline in American democracy, the first issue has to be the measure. The continued disengagement of Americans from the political system is the subject of significant research. Supporting Putnam's approach are broad measures of participation. We are witnessing declining participation, declining voting patterns, and lower rates of belief in the system (Rosenstone and Hansen 1993). In short, the American democratic model is threatened and many view the likely future with pessimism based on these trends. We propose that the Internet may be the solution to reconnecting society. Scholars have theorized that institutional structure can lead to lower rates of turnout and participation. More directly, the volume of elections at multiple levels hurts both the ability of citizens to stay informed as well as their ability to remain engaged. People vote because they wish to influence public policy, so elections with low electoral salience result in low turnout (Franklin 1996). Low turnout can be the product of an institutional structure which inhibits turnout and leads to socioeconomic factors playing a larger role (Powell 1986).

In Putnam's view, social capital is part of the solution to the institutional limitations on participation. When people are engaged with their neighbors and invested in their communities, there is a greater willingness to bear the burden and costs associated with participation even where the elections have lower salience and greater frequency. The declining social capital is leading to less participation (Putnam 1995a, 1995b, 2000). In fact, this isolation thesis is not limited to civic groups but is suggested to be a cause of declining turnout because of the nature of political campaigns. Gerber and Green (2000) assert that turnout decline is the result of lower amounts of face-to-face mobilization, not mobilization in general. The modern campaign which is dominated by television and exposure to negative advertising reduces intention to vote and lowers political efficacy (Ansolabehere et al. 1994).

We suggest that this literature misses the changing nature of society itself and fails to measure nontraditional means of communication. By reconnecting not just people and information, but people to people, the Internet re-creates the missing elements in the participation model. The Internet campaign changes the dynamic of the election. By increasing the volume of information that is easily accessible, it changes the nature and scope of institutional limitations. The difficulty in becoming informed is reduced, making turnout and participation more likely. More directly, if the cost in time and effort of elections are keeping people from participating, the cost savings of the online community can and should reverse that trend among the most adept Internet users, and increase overall participation as the technology penetrates larger groups. Finally, the Internet bypasses the negative campaign model by offering an alternative to the sound-bite approach that can be both comprehensive and interactive. Early studies suggest that if targeted and presented correctly, the Internet has the potential to reverse the regular disinterest among younger voters (Lupia and Philpot 2007). The Internet is such a versatile medium that advances such as Web 2.0 allow users to not only choose the content they would like to access, but also to create the user experience with the content of choice delivered in multiple formats ranging from text to video, and even to multilayered discussion forums. The conversation and interaction on the Internet can vary widely based on the device used and the demands or desires of the users. It can range from the dissemination of short messages using Twitter, to lengthy and responsive blog postings, to video messages using websites like YouTube, or even social websites like Facebook where fan pages and status updates can become forums for political debate or just information sharing.

Putnam suggests that in rebuilding social capital through civic engagement the decline in participation can be curtailed. Yet, Putnam's scope of participation is too limited. The Internet can be the venue for modern social capital. While bowling leagues may have been the means for social networking at one time, the absence of bowling leagues does not mean the absence of networking. Bowling is no longer the focus of the social network, the online community, which is not only fostered but is often hosted by candidates, and which serves many of the same functions of the traditional Putnam model. The Internet hosts thousands of online communities and despite initial commercial beliefs, the Internet is much more frequently used as a means to interact and communicate than as a place to purchase goods and services (Horrigan 2001). Critical to Putnam's argument is that social networking stimulates social capital through building trust. Best and Krueger (2006) present clear evidence that online networking is related to common indicators of social capital, such as generalized trust, but their focus is not to look at how this trust may encourage civic engagement. Krueger (2002) does present empirical evidence that the Internet shows real potential to bring new individuals into the political process. Conversely, research has also suggested that the Internet has done very little to change the traditional have and have-not participation divide (Schlozman, Verba, and Brady 2010). None of these studies measure the connection between political participation and social capital building as a result of social networking through Web 2.0 applications such as Facebook, MySpace, and Twitter. We explore this possibility below.

MEASURING THE NEW PARTICIPATION MODEL

The following analyses have several purposes, but are primarily designed to explore how online social networking affects political participation. First, differences in means tests are used to explore the varying frequency of Internet social networking across behavioral indicators such as civic attentiveness and party identification. These tests are also used to look at the potential variation across demographics such as age, education, income, race, and gender. Second, Internet social networking is modeled as a function of these variables. Third, political participation[2] is modeled as a function of Internet social networking, campaign contact,[3] civic attentiveness, age, education, income, and race. In these models we account for variables other than social networking that might present viable alternative explanations of political participation to help assure that the predicted effects are not spurious.[4] Thus, other than a positive relationship between Internet social networking and participation, we also expect one with campaign contact, civic attentiveness, age, education, and income, and we expect racial minorities to be less likely to participate. Again, the idea that social networking via the Internet may stimulate participation is not novel, but our approach to actually estimating the influence is. Fourth, we constructed models of vote choice. These are purely exploratory. We had no real theoretical reason to expect heightened Internet social networking to be related to vote choice but we decided to explore this question as this is a relatively new area of inquiry. We control for party identification, race, and gender.[5] All analysis using the Pew Data in this chapter is performed only on those who claimed to use the Internet at least occasionally.

It was clear in the descriptive statistics presented in chapter 2 that the young people represented in the Student Data were far more likely to use the Internet as a social networking tool. Given that young people are far more likely to network on the Internet, we should expect generational effects across time.[6] As older generations are replaced by younger generations who are more likely to social network via the Internet, we could potentially see political participation rise over time. Of course, older people are more likely to participate in politics than younger people, but as younger generations become older it is possible that their heightened social networking via the Internet may magnify the increased likelihood of voting based on their age. In short, the two variables may work together, resulting in rising aggregate levels of participation. The findings presented in this section indicate that the pervasiveness of Internet social networking varies across several groups in addition to age cohorts.

Internet social networking across demographics and behavioral indicators does impact political participation as well. Heightened social networking in some groups exacerbates participation differences that already exist. Also, as mentioned above, it lessens differences across some groups such as age cohorts. Just as we did in chapter 3 with information gathering via the Internet, we explore differences in Internet social networking across civic attentiveness, party identification, age, education, income, parents' finances, race, and gender. The results suggest some stark differences across these groups.

The results in table 5.1 are t-tests for a difference of means across the dichotomous independent variables and one-way ANOVA tests for ordinal and non-dichotomous nominal independent variables. All results in this chapter are based on respondents who gave an affirmative answer when asked if they use the Internet at least occasionally. First, one-way ANOVA tests indicate that those who are more attentive to public affairs are more likely to social network than the less attentive in both the Pew and Student Data. In measuring networking online, we were careful to include in our indicator index

Table 5.1. Differences in Social Networking on the Internet

	2008 Pew Data			2008 Student Data		
	Mean	S.D.	P-value	Mean	S.D.	P-value
Civic Attentiveness						
Never	0.53	0.92		—	—	
Hardly at all	0.50	0.82		1.18	0.80	
Only now and then	0.89	1.11		1.60	1.00	
Some of the time	0.89	1.10		1.78	1.17	
Most of the time	1.21	1.26	0.00	2.28	1.25	0.00
Party Identification						
Republican	0.83	1.08		1.87	1.08	
Democrat	0.97	1.18		1.98	1.26	
Independent	0.86	1.11	0.09	1.65	1.08	0.04
Age						
18–29	1.16	1.30		1.84	1.18	
30–39	0.82	1.05		1.49	1.29	
40–49	0.68	0.95		0.92	0.37	
50–59	0.57	0.85		0.20	0.00	
60 and up	—	—	0.00	0.20	0.00	0.14
Education						
H.S. Incomplete	0.49	0.79		—	—	
H.S. Graduate	0.54	0.95		—	—	
Some College/Associate	0.78	1.14		—	—	
College Graduate	1.15	1.15	0.00	—	—	
Income						
Less than $10,000	0.82	1.21		—	—	
$10,000–$20,000	0.96	1.13		—	—	
$20,000–$30,000	0.59	0.97		—	—	
$30,000–$40,000	0.78	1.23		—	—	
$40,000–$50,000	0.75	1.02		—	—	
$50,000–$75,000	0.98	1.30		—	—	
$75,000–$100,000	0.89	1.07		—	—	
$100,000 or more	0.91	1.03	0.00	—	—	—
Parents' Finances						
Poor	—	—		1.72	1.38	
Middle	—	—		1.82	1.19	
Well Off	—	—	—	1.87	1.11	0.67
Race						
White	0.85	1.10		1.83	1.18	
Black	0.85	1.10		1.90	1.18	
Latino	1.20	1.23		1.54	1.10	
Asian	1.04	1.32		1.77	1.22	
Other	0.93	1.41	0.31	1.95	1.29	0.50
Gender						
Male	0.87	1.12		1.75	1.23	
Female	0.89	1.12	0.70	1.89	1.13	0.13
Number of Cases	1626	666				

Note: Data come from the Pew Internet & American Life Project, August 2008 Civic Engagement Survey, and a 2008 survey of college students at the University of Louisville and Florida Atlantic University. P-values represent the probability that we cannot reject the null hypothesis that there is no difference in the magnitude of political Internet use across all above independent variables (T-tests for dichotomous independent variables and one-way ANOVA tests—between groups—for ordinal and non-dichotomous nominal independent variables).

the use of prominent websites or protocols like Facebook and Twitter which may be used for politics, but are primarily social outlets. These outlets are part of the increasingly important movement to Web 2.0 which allows users to define or even create their own web experience. Previously we have found that those who are more attentive are more likely to politically participate. If social networking also leads to engagement, the effect on participation may be magnified by the combination of the two. The pervasiveness of social networking is not high in the Pew Data but nonetheless the highest value of social networking is among those who pay the highest attention to public affairs. In contrast, social networking is common in the Student Data. The mean score for Internet social networking among those who pay attention to public affairs most of the time is 2.28. This is near the midpoint of the index demonstrating that these attentive students are, for the most part, all doing some kind of networking on the Internet. For that matter, even the least attentive are likely to be doing some networking via the Internet.

There is some divergence in the findings across the datasets when it comes to party identification. In the Pew Data, there are no significant differences across party identification. In the Student Data, Democrats score highest (1.98), followed by Republicans (1.87), and then Independents (1.65). Again the numbers are substantially higher among the young people represented in the Student Data. This could have implications for participation as older cohorts are replaced. If younger Democrats are more likely to social network via the Internet and those who network are more likely to participate, we could see a participation gap across party identification as older cohorts are replaced by younger ones. Interestingly, the Student Data suggest that there are no significant differences across age cohorts regarding who is more likely to network. However, in the Pew Data, the younger cohorts participate at higher and more significant rates in social networking. These results only include those respondents who responded affirmatively when asked if they use the Internet at least occasionally. Young people are far more likely to respond affirmatively ($p < 0.00$). Yet, even among those who use the Internet, younger people in the Pew Data are the more likely to use social networks. The growth in the use of networking websites like Facebook is driving this finding. The lack of significance in the Student Data may well be the influence of education which is also correlated with networking, as we will see below.

The differences in means are significant across education and income in the Pew Data. The more educated and those with higher incomes are more likely to social network on the Internet than their respective counterparts. The income differences are not of a significant magnitude until the upper income categories ($75,000 or more). The differences on education are quite stark. The means rise considerably for those with some college and with greater levels of education. These variables were not measured in the Student Data because they are fairly constant. We did attempt to measure income by asking about parents' finances and the differences were not significant. The differences across race are not significant in either dataset, but again blacks and Latinos are significantly less likely to use the Internet generally ($p < 0.01$). Internet use for gaining social capital has a more pronounced effect for certain groups.

Many of these effects hold up in a multivariate setting, but simultaneously controlling for each leads to changes. The results are presented in table 5.2. In the Pew Data, civic attentiveness, education, and age are still significant but income becomes insignificant (and most of the other insignificant predictors remain so). This suggests that the income effects were spurious. The variation in Internet social networking explained by income can be explained away by the variation in civic attentiveness and education. The significant effects indicate that social networking on the Internet increases with civic attentiveness and education *ceteris paribus*. There are also some changes in the Student Data results. Party identification also becomes insignificant suggesting that the results are spurious. Civic attentiveness and age remain significant positively and negatively, respectively. Interestingly, parents' finances and gender become significant in the multivariate setting. The results suggest that Internet social networking is higher among those whose parents earn more and among females. Again, this has interesting implications considering that the sample is comprised of primarily young people. We may expect the proposed effect on participation to have a varied effect on different groups across time.

While it is important and interesting to explore variation in Internet social networking, more central to our theory in this chapter is examining the relationship between networking and political participation. The results contained in table 5.3 indicate that heightened Internet social networking does indeed significantly predict participation in both datasets. This is a more significant finding than simply predicting the likelihood of voting.

Table 5.2. Models of Social Networking on the Internet

	Pew Data		
	Estimate	S.E.	P-Value
Civic Attentiveness	0.32	0.04	0.00
Republican	-0.17	0.11	0.11
Age	-0.47	0.04	0.00
Education	0.64	0.06	0.00
Income	0.02	0.03	0.46
Black	-0.18	0.18	0.32
Latino	0.45	0.21	0.03
Female	0.16	0.10	0.09
-2 Log Likelihood	38429.62		
Nagelkerke Pseudo R^2	0.21		
Number of Cases	1626		
	Student Data		
Civic Attentiveness	0.58	0.07	0.00
Republican	0.05	0.16	0.77
Age	-0.67	0.21	0.00
Parents' Finances	0.23	0.12	0.05
Black	0.25	0.22	0.25
Latino	-0.09	0.28	0.74
Female	0.40	0.14	0.00
-2 Log Likelihood	2621.13		
Nagelkerke Pseudo R^2	0.12		
Number of Cases	666		

Note: Data come from the Pew Internet & American Life Project, August 2008 Civic Engagement Survey, and a 2008 survey of college students at the University of Louisville and Florida Atlantic University. Table entries are ordered logit estimates, associated standard errors, and 95% confidence intervals. Operationalization descriptions are all in chapter 2.

We measure political participation broadly, including participating in rallies and protests, giving speeches, petitioning government, and volunteering in campaigns. Despite this, the Internet was a significant predictor of political participation. Importantly, these findings hold up even when controlling for several theoretical predictors of political participation. The Pew and Student model predicts a significant positive relationship with, as stated above, Internet social networking, and also with campaign contact,[7] civic attentiveness, age, and education, *ceteris paribus*. Surprisingly, the findings on income are mixed. Income is a significant predictor of political participation in the Pew Data, but parents' finances is not a significant predictor in the Student Data. Race has only limited effects in both datasets. Most important to our theory

Table 5.3. Models of Political Participation

	2008 Pew Data		
	Estimate	S.E.	P-value
Internet Networking	0.75	0.05	0.00
Campaign Contact	0.22	0.02	0.00
Civic Attentiveness	0.37	0.04	0.00
Age	0.20	0.04	0.00
Education	0.15	0.06	0.01
Income	0.08	0.02	0.00
Black	-0.04	0.17	0.83
Latino	-0.01	0.20	0.95
–2 Log Likelihood	6044.30		
Nagelkerke Pseudo R^2	0.40		
Number of Cases	1626		
	2008 Student Data		
Internet Networking	0.73	0.15	0.00
Civic Attentiveness	1.06	0.10	0.00
Age	0.64	0.22	0.00
Parents' Finances	0.07	0.25	0.77
Black	-0.49	0.35	0.16
Latino	-0.08	0.14	0.54
–2 Log Likelihood	971.13		
Nagelkerke Pseudo R^2	0.27		
Number of Cases	666		

Note: Data come from the Pew Internet & American Life Project, November 2008 Civic Engagement Survey, and a 2008 survey of college students at the University of Louisville and Florida Atlantic University. Table entries are ordered logit estimates with associated standard errors. **$p \le 0.05$, *$p \le 0.10$.

is that the effect of Internet social networking appears to be independent of both general engagement and external campaign influence in the Pew model, with the demographic controls.

While we have no real theoretical reason to expect that heightened political Internet use would be related to actual vote choice, given that so little is known about how the Internet is affecting people's political perspectives, it is a question worth exploring. Thus, we modeled whether or not one voted for more Democratic candidates versus Republican candidates as a function of Internet social networking, party identification, race, and gender. Interestingly, Internet social networking is significant in the Pew model and in the Student model. Both models suggest that the more people use the Internet for social networking the more likely they are to vote for Democrats. This suggests that the Democrats have an early advantage in using the Internet to mobilize support among young networkers and networkers in general. The Pew model is likely influenced by the efforts of the Obama campaign to mobilize online resources with a greater intensity and effect than the competing McCain campaign. The Obama campaign used multiple methods of online social networking with unprecedented success. There were multiple Facebook groups supporting the Obama campaign, which is not particularly noteworthy until the magnitude of the groups is seen. In just one of the many student groups the Obama campaign had, 3.2 million networkers signed up (Vargas 2008). The Obama campaign had a vast network of online donors regularly recruited from social networking protocols such as Twitter and websites, including Facebook and many others, which allowed them to assemble millions of e-mail addresses from which to solicit money and support (Vargas 2008).

Nonetheless, it is problematic for us to generalize with these data. In 2008, there was a clear advantage to the Democrats in the use of online campaigning and the appeal to social networkers, but it is far too early to predict a long-term partisan benefit. Yet, there is a developing pattern among young educated people that initially favors the Democrats, as can be seen in table 5.4. Those with education are more likely to vote, so as older generations are replaced, these data would suggest that those replacing them could give gains to the Democrats. Party identification and race are significant in both models, but gender is not. As expected, Democrats and African Americans are more likely to vote for Democrats. As a result of the significance of these variables, we can be confident that the effects of Internet social networking in the Student model are not spurious. As more elections are conducted in the Internet age, a larger pattern will emerge to see whether the advantage wielded by the Democrats in the 2008 election is sustained.

CONCLUSION

The findings presented in this chapter suggest several things. First, there is some variation across political variables and standard demographics when it comes to who is more likely to social network via the Internet. In addition, there is some evidence that heightened Internet social networking is related to vote choice, at least among young people represented in the Student Data and in the 2008 election. While this is interesting, the most important finding in this study is that Internet social networking is positively associated

Table 5.4.   Models of Vote Choice

	Pew Data		
	Estimate	S.E.	P-value
Internet Networking	0.36	0.06	0.00
Democrat	3.15	0.19	0.00
Independent	1.90	0.19	0.00
Black	1.33	0.25	0.00
Female	0.15	0.13	0.25
–2 Log Likelihood	1515.46		
Nagelkerke Pseudo R^2	0.41		
Number of Cases	1683		
	Student Data		
Internet Networking	0.27	0.10	0.01
Party Identification (7-point)	0.78	0.06	0.00
Black	0.70	0.40	0.08
Female	0.08	0.21	0.70
–2 Log Likelihood	571.423		
Nagelkerke Pseudo R^2	0.52		
Number of Cases	666		

Note: Data come from the Pew Internet & American Life Project, August 2008 Civic Engagement Survey, and a 2008 survey of college students at the University of Louisville and Florida Atlantic University. Table entries are logit estimates, associated standard errors, and 95% confidence intervals. Operationalization descriptions are all in chapter 2.

with political participation. This finding provides hard empirical evidence in support of conjecture in previous work suggesting that the Internet actually represents a new means of building social capital, which in turn can stimulate political participation.

While these findings are revealing, more needs to be done to make this relationship clearer. It would also be interesting to see if more or less social capital is built across the different ways that people use the Internet. Do networking sites have a greater effect than the exchange of information through e-mail, are videos more influential than written communication, and are blogs more influential than traditional news? These are all questions that can still be explored. For now, it can be clearly stated that there is a relationship between political Internet use generally and the propensity to vote and participate.

6

The Internet

Two One-Sided Information Flows?

Of late, there has been a great deal of debate about whether public opinion in the United States has become increasingly polarized. Pundits such as Fox's Bill O'Reilly claim that the United States is polarized as a result of an existing culture war between "traditionalists" and "secular-progressives" (O'Reilly 2006). Alternatively, some political scientists such as Morris P. Fiorina claim that the polarization of America is a myth (Fiorina, Abrams, and Pope 2006), suggesting that most Americans are fairly moderate and generally agree on those issues thought to be most divisive. The extent of the polarization in the United States is beyond the scope of this book, and likely could not be settled here regardless. Yet, the Internet does have an important and perhaps determinative role in this discussion. The very nature of the Internet reinforces some of the basic tendency to polarize. As a result, we suggest that the Internet, as the newest form of media, may be contributing to an increasingly more polarized America with each side restricted, increasingly by choice, to confined regions of the Internet.

Much of our current understanding of the psychological processes associated with political public opinion comes from John Zaller's (1992) seminal work, *The Nature and Origins of Mass Opinion*. In that work, Zaller asserts that change and stability in public opinion is driven, in part, by shifts in what he calls "two-sided information flows." As one might surmise, media influences what issues or events are at the forefront for many, if not most, people. Zaller takes these concepts and argues that on most issues the popular media present two different sides of each issue, usually from ideologically liberal and conservative positions. This is generally referred to as a two-sided information flow. This distribution of information shapes the considerations or information that individuals judge when reaching decisions, especially political decisions. This has an important effect on people. The attitudes of each person and their expressed opinions are made up of a wide range of considerations. People will review these considerations and from them draw an attitude which averages across them. Typically, when a person expresses an opinion he or she is thinking about the considerations that were most recently in mind. If only one set of ideas is regularly set forth from the media, it can affect the considerations people use to form attitudes and opinions. As a result, the level of polarization on issues in public opinion is guided by the degree to which the information is one- or two-sided. Counterintuitively, a two-sided information flow can result in polarization because people for both sides have sufficient information to take an ideological position. This is particularly true if the information is available in a way that allows the user to access only one side. One-sided information flows have a depolarizing effect because they stimulate agreement.

Political scientists and even political pundits are well aware of the power the mass media have to influence and even shape public opinion. As a result, the discussion of media biases, especially in television, is prominent (Bennett 2004). Yet, there is broader context to this discussion and larger implications outside the traditional media. The Internet provides more opportunity than traditional media sources for people to acquire one-sided information. Much of that derives from the fact that the Internet is a very open and accessible medium. Unlike television or even newspapers, the content of one's information on the Internet is entirely at the discretion of the user. In fact, with the growth of Web 2.0, which allows the user to customize the images they see and the information they access, this trend is accelerating. The Internet provides an incalculable choice of information. If people prefer a particular bias, it is readily available in abundance on the Internet. While the Internet is freer and more accessible than any media or medium in history, users can use it to avoid anything with which they may disagree or simply choose not see.

Understood in this context, the Internet has a great potential to polarize people by offering readily available one-sided information combined with an interface, like Web 2.0, which easily rewards a preference for such informa-tion. This structure by its nature will interrupt the uneven, but generally two-sided, information flows from the modern media. As a result, the Internet may create an increasingly polarized public. Many Americans are ambivalent about a range of issues as a result of two-sided information flows (Zaller 1992). The Internet can transform this ambivalence into more one-sided opinions as it increasingly becomes people's primary source of information. As people acquire less conflicting information by relying on news sources and blogs that share their point of view, they have less cognitive conflict, less ambivalence, and the nation as a whole may become more polarized. This phenomenon has tremendous implications for American democracy. Yet, this future is not as bleak as it would seem. Even though it is more contentious, a polarized electorate can actually stimulate participation in the process, along with debate over the issues.

To analyze the implications of the Internet on the flow of information, we return to the Pew Data to address several questions. First, to what degree do people prefer and seek out one-sided information? Second, do those who prefer one-sided information gather political information via the Internet at higher rates than those who do not? Third, who is more likely to seek out one-sided information such as biased news sites, blogs, and candidate websites? Fourth, do those who prefer one-sided information actually seek out one-sided information sources more than those who do not? And finally, what are the current electoral implications?

The results of the analyses presented here suggest that the Internet is clearly impacting the type of information many are acquiring. Initially, while most claimed to prefer information that presents multiple views, a large segment of the population actually prefers information that shares their point of view. As people are less likely to self-report personal bias, it's not surprising that most claim to be evenhanded in their search for information. Yet many are willing to concede that they seek out one-sided information. Further, the findings indicate that those who prefer one-sided information are gathering informa-tion via the Internet at higher rates than those who do not. Interestingly, the data show that there are behavioral and demographic indicators that affect the kinds of sources people prefer when seeking one-sided information (bi-ased news sites, blogs, and candidate websites). Those who prefer one-sided information, not surprisingly, are seeking it out at higher rates than those who do not. Finally, and most pertinent to the implications of the disruption of two-sided information flows, those who seek out one-sided information are more likely to vote.

Before moving to a more detailed analysis of the data, we must put the changes the Internet causes into a firmer theoretical foundation. We begin with Zaller's (1992) theory of one-sided and two-sided information flows and their relationship to ambivalence, with our additions detailing how the Internet requires an adjustment to his theory. In doing so, we expound on our base formulation concerning how the Internet may contribute to a polarized public. Second, we discuss the extant literature that has explored the differences in traditional media and Internet media. This discussion highlights how these differences influence the information flow. Finally, we detail our argument that the Internet is revolutionizing American politics by polarizing public opinion and, in turn, stimulating participation. The results are then presented followed by a discussion of the normative implications of these findings.

ONE TWO-SIDED INFORMATION FLOW OR
TWO ONE-SIDED INFORMATION FLOWS?

Zaller (1992) begins his treatment of the influence of the flow of information through the media by exploring one-sided communications. Using survey data from the American National Election Studies, he demonstrates that contextual changes in the flow of information correlate with shifts in public opinion. For example, he shows that the generally one-sided (negative) coverage of elite discourse surrounding the Iran-Contra scandal in the 1980s corresponded with dropping evaluations of President Reagan. He observes that as elite discourse as covered in the popular media becomes more partisan or ideological, there is a polarizing effect in public opinion. Zaller models this effect and proposes that the stability of public opinion is largely dependent on whether communication flows are one-sided or evenly balanced. He notes that, in most cases, there is not a one-sided message but rather there is usually a dominant message and a countervailing message. People's resistance of the dominant message is largely dependent on the relative intensities of the messages along with the presence of a countervailing message, and their own personal characteristics such as ideological predisposition, political awareness, and values. As a result, a two-sided information flow that has relative equal intensity from both sides should lead to a polarized public.

We argue that the Internet can disrupt the two-sided information flow for individuals, making the resistance to dominant or countervailing views unnecessary, based primarily on the ease in self-selecting the media information on the Internet. One-sided information can be selected at virtually no cost. There may still be a two-sided information flow in the traditional media outlets but the Internet, despite its inherent diversity, allows people the opportunity to ignore one side. As a medium, the Internet provides this difference in a much different way than a broadcast television network or a national magazine. While one can search through a newspaper for one-sided information, the stream of information presented by traditional journalists is largely two-sided by design. Most mainstream media are seeking the largest audience and thus must have a broad appeal. The Internet operates with no such constraint. While there are two-sided websites, most of those are outposts of traditional sources such as newspapers or television networks. The vast growth in Internet webpages is not constrained by a desire for broad appeal and can be narrowly focused to a select audience. Even those sources seeking a larger audience can find it with one-sided information, based on the unprecedented distribution potential of the Internet.

When considered in the context of the Internet, the effect of one-sided information should be even more significant. Because of the nature of how the Internet transmits information by demand, polarization is magnified. Traditional media are one-sided or two-sided on any particular issue. The Internet creates an alternative environment where there are two one-sided information flows. We suggest that the Internet, as it relates to American politics, presents two distinct and identifiable views of political information, a liberal one and a conservative one. This is a clear contrast to the single two-sided information flow from traditional media sources. A one-sided information flow should result in polarization as each side reads and learns in isolation and in the absence of alternate view points. It creates zones for each side, creating even greater polarization than any one traditional media can do even if it is overtly biased. Theories of cognitive dissonance (Festinger 1957) suggest that holding conflicting views is uncomfortable for individuals. Thus, they inherently try to avoid conflict and seek out information consistent with their existing worldview. Reviewing media sources that are consistent with persisting belief systems reinforces those beliefs and attitudes, making compromise or neutral positions increasingly unlikely. Considerations are shaped by the information the media make available. If one-sided information is available, many are likely to be inclined to get this type of information because it reduces cognitive dissonance.

Beyond reinforcing existing cleavages, the one-sided flows of information from the Internet are likely to move more people out of a neutral position on political issues. When people have strongly held beliefs, they seek to confirm them with their choice in media. For people who have no firm belief concerning an issue, two-sided flows of information are conflicting and can leave them undecided or neutral. Internal conflict over political issues is not always resolved and the result is ambivalence, or the simultaneous possession of positive and negative evaluations of a single attitude object (Alvarez and Brehm 1995; Eagly and Chaiken 1993; Zaller 1992; Zaller and Feldman 1992; see Craig and Martinez 2005a, 2005b for a complete review of ambivalence). The availability of one-sided information from the Internet should decrease ambivalence among individuals; thus, aggregate polarization should increase. If people continue to gather information from the Internet, their sources will increasingly be one-sided. As a result, they will not have as much conflicting information cognitively accessible. In turn they will not see a conflict and, based on which source they rely on, will join one position or the other. Fewer individuals will be ambivalent as the Internet begins to dominate the distribution of political views and news. If the gathering of one-sided information is proportionate to ideological predispositions in the public, those predispositions will be reinforced, resulting in a more intensely polarized public.

While we expect the effect of these implications to be measurable, the initial impact should be more limited as the Internet has not become the dominant distribution network we expect it will be in future years. Nonetheless, we assert that people are gathering one-sided information, and this is happening at rates high enough to make a difference concerning polarization even if this phenomenon is only in its early stages. Most are still relying on traditional sources of media; thus, Zaller's theory of one two-sided information flow is still dominant. We contend that as older generations are replaced with younger ones who rely on the Internet for news, aggregate ambivalence will decrease and polarization will increase. The next section addresses the literature that has explored the nature of Internet media. Is it actually a source of two one-sided information flows and are people relying on these one-sided flows for their information?

THE NEW MEDIA

It is reasonable to expect that the political news that citizens select to consume is largely determined by the available choices. Since the advent of the Internet, the breadth of the possible choices has considerably broadened. There have been conflicting views surrounding the potential implications of this development. On one side, research has indicated that while the breadth of outlets has increased, the most popular news sites on the Internet are owned and operated by the same major conglomerates that run the major television and print outlets, along with news aggregators (Freedman 2006; Sparks 2000; Stanyer 2008). News aggregators compile material from other news agencies; so, much of it comes from traditional outlets. They do not produce their own content. This static view of the Internet suggests that other than convenience, the Internet has done little to change the content of information that people acquire because it is all coming from the same outlets as traditional sources. If this is the case, we would likely expect a typical two-sided information flow as opposed to two one-sided flows because journalists from traditional outlets try to maintain some kind of "objectivity" based on a code of journalistic ethics, and management/ownership generally prefers this approach so that they may reach a wider audience (Bennett 2004). Most empirical research has not identified significant ideological bias in the reporting from mainstream outlets such as network news and major newspapers (Bennett 2004).

While it may be the case that some of the new Internet media is just an extension of the mainstream television and print outlets, that view is a limited and static understanding of the Internet that becomes less true as time passes. It also ignores the interactive nature of the Internet environment. Other research has challenged the static model by suggesting that the Internet provides echo chambers where like-minded people are exposed to one-sided arguments that reinforce their initial predispositions (Davis 1999; Hill and Hughes 1998; Wilhelm 2000; Wojcieszak 2006). Further, research has also contended that discussion on the Internet is primarily comprised of interactions with like-minded people (Sunstein 2001; Van Alstyne and Brynjolfsson 1995). Rainie and Horrigan (2007) present critical findings supporting the move of people away from online outposts of traditional media outlets. Their analysis of Pew Data found that of those who use the Internet, over 50 percent obtained information about the 2006 congressional election from non-traditional sources. Further, Patterson (2007) finds that usage of sites connected to non-traditional news organizations is growing faster than those connected to traditional organizations. He did include news aggregators as non-traditional but also finds that usage of "aggregators with attitude" or partisan aggregators is rapidly growing. His results also suggest that blog sites are growing faster than traditional news organization sites. Pew Data illustrates that a quarter of those who use the Internet used blogs to gather information in 2006, which was up 60 percent from 2004 (Rainie and Horrigan 2007). Thus, there is some compelling evidence that many are being exposed to sites that are more inclined to present one-sided information flows and the trend is favoring those non-traditional outlets.

The Internet also enables people to avoid broader surveys of the news for increasingly specific and focused distributions and analysis of an issue. Specialization, the desire for news and information focused on one smaller issue, lends itself to one-sided information flows. If they are able, people tend to focus their attention on specific topics (Tewksbury and Rittenberg 2008). Tewksbury (2005) finds evidence that many who use the Internet to gather news information tend to select specific topics when they go online. Some argue that specialization leads to fragmentation of the public. Fragmentation exists when public exposure to any given topic is not widespread (Tewksbury and Rittenberg 2008). Essentially, people are self-selecting content based on their interests and this fragments the shared knowledge of topics. If people are fragmenting and gathering one-sided information when they do so, from either side, one likely consequence is polarization (Webster and Phalen 1997).

As described earlier, we argue that the Internet is indeed contributing to polarization. The question is, how widespread is this phenomenon? We contend that the impact is just beginning and propose that it is likely to be exacerbated. First, as stated above, usage of independent, ideological news sites and blogs is rapidly growing. These sources are contributing to one-sided information flows. There have always been alternative sources of information but the cost of acquiring information from these sources is significantly reduced as a result of the Internet. Simply, much of it is free and is only a click away. Second, younger people are more likely to use the Internet as their primary source of news (see chapter 3), and just based on the increased availability of one-sided information sources, we should expect higher proportions of those who use the Internet as their primary source, relative to those who do not, to gather information from such sources. Thus, polarization is likely to magnify as older people in the population are replaced by younger ones.

Combining the arguments that like-minded people are exposed to one-sided arguments, the public is specializing and fragmenting, the Internet lowers the cost of gathering one-sided information, and finally, the population is being replaced with more frequent users of the Internet, we contend that the Internet is contributing and will contribute in the future to a polarization of public opinion. If this is the case, it leads us to the question of political implications. In the next section, we address one potential implication. We grapple with the possibility that one-sided information flows may contribute to a transformation in how people behave and participate in the political system.

INFORMATION FLOWS AND POLITICAL PARTICIPATION

While the Internet will ultimately alter the calculus concerning why and how people participate in the political system, we do not reject the well-studied analysis of the socioeconomic drivers of political participation. There are several schools of thought when it comes to explaining why people participate in the political process. Verba, Schlozman, and Brady (1995) summarized these schools of thought into what they called the "civic volunteerism model." This model puts the different influences on participation into three broad categories. They are: 1) personal characteristics, 2) group effects, and 3) political attitudes. To this, we add campaign mobilization (whether or not one was contacted by a campaign). Political scientists stress education and income when it comes to personal characteristics that stimulate participation. The argument is not that income and education directly encourage participation, but rather income and education help develop the skills and orientations that facilitate the ability to engage the system (Nie, Junn, and Stehlik-Barry 1996; Verba, Schlozman, and Brady 1995). Other personal characteristics such as gender (Norris 2002) and race (Leighley and Vedlitz 1999; Verba et al. 1993) may also influence the propensity to participate. Finally, political attitudes may include a range of things such as issue attitudes, psychological attachment to a political party, and political attentiveness. Our contribution here is to this last category. We propose that one-sided information flows via the Internet may actually stimulate political participation by influencing political attitudes such as partisan attachment and ideology.

Attitudes are a mix of positive and negative considerations (Zaller 1992). As described earlier, these considerations are largely shaped by the flow of information through the media. The Internet as a source of information is disrupting a two-sided information flow at the individual level, resulting in two one-sided flows wherein many are not being exposed to two-sided information, or at least their exposure is limited. It is our contention that this crystallization of attitudes actually stimulates participation. People who are ambivalent or confused about issues or candidates are much more likely to avoid participating. The Internet by its aggregate polarizing effect creates more partisans who are more likely participants, if only to rally for one's side and defeat the opposition.

Specifically, partisanship and ideology can be conceptualized as attitudes. They are psychological attachments to sets of ideas. These attachments may be crystallized as a result of the consumption of one-sided information. People's range of considerations is shaped by the information they consume. If this information is largely one-sided (liberal or conservative, pro-Democrat or pro-Republican), the likely result is a strengthening of the predisposition. As a result, these one-sided information flows may simultaneously encourage satisfaction with the side being positively presented and dissatisfaction with the other side. Satisfaction and dissatisfaction with government can encourage participation (Dalton 2006). For instance, those satisfied may vote to continue the government's current direction and those dissatisfied to change it. Further, there is evidence that ideological extremists and strong partisans are more likely to participate (Dalton 2006). Summarized, one-sided information flows can crystallize attitudes, attitudes are a predictor of participation, and the Internet offers a great deal of one-sided information. Thus, the new media will likely result in greater participation.

METHODS

The following analyses using the 2006 and 2008 Pew Post-Election Data have several purposes.[1] First, we graphically present the frequency distribution of preference for non-biased or two-sided news (see chapter 2). Second, we estimate an ordered logit model of Internet information gathering as a function of preference of non-biased or two-sided news, controlling for the significant predictors of the model of Internet information gathering in chapter 3. This permits us to determine if those who prefer non-biased news are gathering information via the Internet at lower rates. Third, we look at the frequency distribution of usage of one-sided sites and then explore differences of such across a range of demographic variables and attentiveness to public affairs. Attentiveness to public affairs is excluded in the 2008 analyses because that variable was not available. Fourth, we estimate ordered logit models of this usage as a function of Internet information gathering, preference for non-biased news, and a dummy variable representing whether the Internet is one's primary source of news, and control for the above range of demographic variables and attentiveness to public affairs. Finally, we estimate logit models of participation for 2006 and 2008 (participation operationalization is included in the appendix). The models estimate political participation (intent to vote) as a function of usage of one-sided sites, campaign contact, civic attentiveness (2006 only), age, education, income, and race. The idea here is to control for explanations of participation alternative to preference for non-biased news to help assure that the predicted effects are not spurious.[2]

RESULTS

The entire argument in this chapter hinges on the premise that people will consume one-sided information if the Internet makes it more readily available. Based on Zaller's (1992) theory, the result should be less cognitive conflict at the individual level. We then extend this argument, suggesting that polarization at the aggregate level is a potential consequence because two crystallized camps are likely through self-selection of news. Significant numbers of citizens would need to actually be consuming one-sided information for this to be the case. Recall that the results presented in figure 2.6 suggest that a sizable chunk of the public claims to prefer news that shares their point of view (near 31 percent). To build on our argument here, we estimate the effect of news preference on Internet information gathering. The results lend further support to the contention that this preference is, indeed, consequential. The model presented in table 6.1 shows that those who prefer news that does not have a point of view (two-sided information) actually gathered less information via the Internet in 2006 and 2008, *ceteris paribus*.[3] This has significant implications. If those who prefer one-sided information are gathering information at higher rates via the Internet than those who do not, the polarization effect is actually magnified as a result of the readily available one-sided information sources. Essentially, the Internet sets up the potential for those who prefer one-sided information to assure the crystalliza-tion of their attitude.

Table 6.1 also illustrates some additional effects. Not surprisingly, those whose primary source of news is the Internet were gathering information via the Internet at higher rates in 2006 and 2008. Also, people with higher civic attention (2006) and income were gathering more information on the Internet (2006 and 2008). There were mixed results regarding age and educa-tion. They were only significant in the 2008 model. The results suggested that older people are less likely to gather information from the Internet and that the more educated are more likely to do so. Taken altogether, this provides an opportunity for the creation and maintenance of narrow, yet active and engaged civic and political groups to thrive. Aided by increasingly one-sided cable media news, the Internet provides a forum for groups to form around a consistent and undisputed set of ideas and information with the one-sided

Table 6.1.   Internet Information Gathering as a Function of News Preference

	2006 Pew Data			
	Estimate	S.E.	95% Confidence Intervals	
Prefer Non-Biased News	−1.06	0.14	−1.34	−0.78
Internet Primary News Source	0.75	0.17	0.43	1.08
Civic Attentiveness	0.50	0.10	0.32	0.69
Age	−0.10	0.05	−0.20	0.01
Education	0.11	0.05	0.00	0.22
Income	0.09	0.04	0.01	0.17
−2 Log Likelihood	2867.38			
Nagelkerke Pseudo R^2	0.18			
Number of Cases	657			
	2008 Pew Data			
Prefer Non-Biased News	−0.89	0.12	−1.13	−0.66
Internet Primary News Source	0.95	0.14	0.68	1.22
Age	−0.09	0.04	−0.18	−0.01
Education	0.20	0.04	0.11	0.29
Income	0.12	0.03	0.05	0.19
−2 Log Likelihood	3501.27			
Nagelkerke Pseudo R^2	0.15			
Number of Cases	918			

Note: Data come from the Pew Internet & American Life Project, November 2006 Post-Election Tracking Survey, and 2008 Civic Engagement Survey. Table entries are ordered logit estimates, associated stan-dard errors, and 95% confidence intervals.

sources on the Internet reinforcing those attitudes and opinions. Political groups like the conservative Tea Party or the alternative liberal groups benefit in membership from the intensity generated by one-sided information that is reinforced and unchallenged in their area of the network.

To explore these implications further, we examined the differences in the frequency with which people are gathering one-sided information across a range of demographics and civic attentiveness. There are not as many interesting differences across groups regarding the frequency of usage of these one-sided sites,[4] but the differences that are significant are particularly illuminating for the participation effect argument that we theorize. First, those who are the most civically attentive are more likely to use one-sided sites to gather information (see table 6.2). Put more simply, the people most involved and engaged in politics are the most likely to seek information from one-sided sources on the Internet (2006). These people represent the same attentive public who are more likely to participate in campaigns and to vote, making their resulting polarization particularly significant. Further, those with higher levels of education, who are also more likely to participate, were also more likely to go to one-sided websites in 2006, but this relationship was not significant in 2008. It is important to remember that these results are all among people who claim to use the Internet to gather political information, so it is not a comparison across the general population. Thus, those with higher education generally are more likely to gather information at higher rates, but this could not be tested because the questions were not asked of everyone.

Other noteworthy findings in this table are the differences across party identification and age. There is not much of a difference for Republicans and Democrats, but surprisingly, Independents in 2006 were significantly more likely to visit one-sided sites (significant at 0.08 in 2006 and 0.01 in 2008). The differences across age only approach significance at the 0.10 level in 2006 and the 0.05 level in 2008, but nevertheless, the conditional means are interesting. It appears that those in the youngest (18–29) and oldest (60 and up) are the most likely to visit one-sided sites. The finding regarding the youngest group lends support to our contention that polarization is likely to increase as older generations are replaced with younger ones, assuming that they continue to visit one-sided sites and that new generations follow suit. The finding regarding the older group is interesting but not problematic. Ultimately the tendencies of the younger generation, if maintained and consistent, will

Table 6.2. Differences of Usage of One-Sided Sites

	2006			2008		
	Mean	S.D.	P-value	Mean	S.D.	P-value
Civic Attentiveness						
Hardly at all	0.50	0.86		—	—	
Only now and then	0.48	0.74		—	—	
Some of the time	0.64	0.91		—	—	
Most of the time	0.94	1.02	0.00	—	—	
Party Identification						
Republican	0.78	0.93		1.28	1.32	
Democrat	0.75	1.00		1.16	1.38	
Independent	0.95	1.02	0.08	1.54	1.44	0.01
Age						
18–29	0.94	1.00		1.52	1.39	
30–39	0.84	1.04		1.43	1.34	
40–49	0.70	0.96		1.36	1.41	
50–59	0.72	0.92		1.34	1.34	
60 and up	0.96	1.01	0.09	—	—	0.06
Education						
None or grades 1–8	—	—		2.00	2.00	
H.S. Incomplete	0.75	0.87		0.73	0.88	
H.S. Graduate	0.67	0.94		1.50	1.33	
Tech School after H.S.	0.47	0.94		1.75	1.29	
Some College/Associates	0.93	1.02		1.39	1.42	
College Graduate	0.70	0.86		1.45	1.44	
Post-Graduate	1.01	1.12	0.02	1.54	1.32	0.32
Income						
Less than $10,000	0.67	1.30		1.38	1.02	
$10,000–$20,000	0.89	1.17		1.40	1.50	
$20,000–$30,000	1.03	1.16		1.25	1.24	
$30,000–$40,000	0.78	0.91		1.70	1.55	
$40,000–$50,000	0.85	1.01		1.38	1.30	
$50,000–$75,000	0.71	0.92		1.41	1.45	
$75,000–$100,000	0.85	0.98		1.43	1.39	
$100,000 or more	0.86	0.99	0.76	1.55	1.34	0.61
Race						
White	0.82	0.98		1.44	1.40	
Black	0.80	1.04		1.68	1.29	
Asian	0.77	1.00		0.94	1.03	
Latino	0.33	0.51		1.52	1.22	
Other	1.13	1.13	0.55	1.88	1.58	0.20
Gender						
Male	0.81	0.98		1.55	0.98	
Female	0.84	1.00	0.64	1.36	1.00	0.05
Number of Cases	657			918		

Note: Data come from the Pew Internet & American Life Project, November 2006 and 2008 Post-Election Tracking Surveys. P-values represent the probability that we cannot reject the null hypothesis that there is no difference in the magnitude of political Internet use across all above independent variables (T-tests for dichotomous independent variables and one-way ANOVA tests—between groups—for ordinal and non-dichotomous nominal independent variables). The mean score for the grades 1–8 category is high for the 2008 data because there was only one case.

replace the older generations over time. There is no statistical difference across race in 2006 or 2008 and no significant difference between the genders in 2006, but in 2008 females were slightly more likely to visit one-sided sites.

We estimated a multivariate model, presented in table 6.3, to see how the findings presented in table 6.2 hold up when controlling for each other. There are some changes. Age becomes insignificant when controlling for other factors. Again, it is important to remember that these results are based on those who did use the Internet to gather political information. Thus, there still is likely an age gap across the general population. Education had no significant effect in 2006, but had a significant and negative effect on seeking one-sided sources in 2008 (p=0.01). It is not clear what role education will have going forward, but it appears possible that a gap may continue. All other controls were insignificant.

More central to our theory of two one-sided information flows and polarization, the model presented in table 6.3 estimates the effects of Internet information gathering, preference for non-biased news, and whether the Internet is one's primary source of news on usage of one-sided sites, *ceteris paribus*. The results presented in table 6.3 provide significant support to our theory. The findings suggest that there is a positive relationship between information gathering via the Internet and usage of one-sided sites even when holding all other things constant. This finding is consistent in both 2006 and 2008. People who use the Internet to inform themselves seem to favor one-sided information.

Importantly, this finding holds up, as do the others, even when controlling for preference for two-sided information, which is also significant. This creates an interesting picture of the electorate. All of the significant results presented in this table are present regardless of whether one's stated preference for information is unbiased. In addition, there is a significant relationship between one's stated primary source of news and usage of one-sided sites. Those who state that the Internet is their primary source of news seem to visit one-sided sites via the Internet more than those who claim some other primary source of news such as newspapers, television, radio, or magazines. Again, it is important to note that these results are only for people who claim to use the Internet at least sometimes to gather political information. Altogether these results clearly suggest that for those who use the Internet as a tool for gathering information, it seems to be predominantly providing a certain type of information—one-sided.

Table 6.3.   Model of Usage of One-Sided Sites

	2006 Pew Data		
	Estimate	S.E	P-value
Internet Information Gathering	0.20	0.03	0.00
Prefer Non-Biased News	-0.71	0.16	0.00
Internet Primary News Source	0.33	0.18	0.07
Civic Attentiveness	0.33	0.12	0.01
Republican	-0.18	0.17	0.29
Age	-0.08	0.06	0.21
Education	0.05	0.06	0.44
Income	-0.07	0.05	0.15
Black	-0.16	0.30	0.60
Latino	0.28	0.38	0.47
Female	0.13	0.16	0.42
–2 Log Likelihood	1448.78		
Nagelkerke Pseudo R^2	0.22		
Number of Cases	657		
	2008 Pew Data		
Internet Information Gathering	0.35	0.02	0.00
Prefer Non-Biased News	-0.87	0.14	0.00
Internet Primary News Source	0.48	0.15	0.00
Republican	-0.28	0.14	0.05
Age	-0.06	0.05	0.25
Education	-0.13	0.05	0.01
Income	0.03	0.04	0.39
Black	0.11	0.24	0.65
Latino	-0.27	0.48	0.57
Female	-0.10	0.13	0.44
–2 Log Likelihood	2443.52		
Nagelkerke Pseudo R^2	0.39		
Number of Cases	918		

Note: Data come from the Pew Internet & American Life Project, November 2006 and 2008 Post-Election Tracking Surveys. Table entries are ordered logit estimates, associated standard errors, and p-values representing the probability that we cannot reject the null hypothesis. Operationalization descriptions are all in chapter 2.

The final models presented in this chapter address one of the potential implications of the consumption of one-sided information. Again, we contend that this consumption, by creating more polarization, may actually stimulate political participation. This is perhaps the most controversial proposition that we make in this chapter. Typically, most view the polarization of politics as negative and disrupting to the political process. Conversely, most think participating in the political process is not only positive, but also an essential requirement for a vibrant and healthy democracy. Yet, our findings support the proposition that the Internet contributes to polarizing public opinion and that this polarization may actually stimulate political participation.

As noted above, ambivalence often results in declines in participation. Conversely, those with crystallized attitudes are more likely to participate.[5] The results presented in table 6.4 suggest that the usage of one-sided sites to gather information is positively associated with the propensity to vote in the 2006 data (p = 0.09). This finding holds up and actually strengthens in 2008 (p = 0.08). We control for the same predictors of participation as we did in

Table 6.4. Models of Political Participation

	2006 Pew Data		
	Estimate	S.E	P-value
One-Sided Site Usage	0.21	0.12	0.09
Campaign Contact	0.47	0.10	0.00
Civic Attentiveness	0.49	0.13	0.00
Age	0.29	0.09	0.00
Black	0.06	0.37	0.89
Latino	−1.13	0.43	0.01
Education	0.35	0.08	0.00
Income	0.01	0.06	0.92
−2 Log Likelihood	539.10		
Nagelkerke Pseudo R^2	0.30		
Number of Cases	657		
	2008 Pew Data		
One-Sided Site Usage	0.20	0.12	0.08
Campaign Contact	0.29	0.07	0.00
Age	0.49	0.12	0.00
Black	1.41	0.41	0.00
Latino	−0.82	0.67	0.22
Education	0.07	0.10	0.48
Income	0.08	0.08	0.28
−2 Log Likelihood	388.82		
Nagelkerke Pseudo R^2	0.22		
Number of Cases	918		

Note: Data come from the Pew Internet & American Life Project, November 2006 and 2008 Post-Election Tracking Surveys. Table entries are logit estimates, associated standard errors, and p-values representing the probability that we cannot reject the null hypothesis. Operationalization descriptions are all in chapter 2.

the participation model in chapter 5 (table 5.3). As one would expect, being contacted by the campaign (2006 and 2008), civic attentiveness (in 2006), education (in 2006), and age (positive relationship) are significant and likely predictors of political participation. Yet, even while controlling for these effects, the usage of one-sided sites to gather information is a positive predictor of political participation. In the end, the evidence presented here clearly suggests that the consumption of one-sided information has real political consequence.

CONCLUSION

The findings in this chapter provide support to our theoretical contention that the Internet is, indeed, potentially disrupting the typical two-sided information flow present in traditional media outlets. The Internet provides increased opportunity for people to select one-sided information for their consumption. This is not inconsequential, as the results presented in this chapter indicate that a significant portion of the public actually prefers their news to share their point of view. The Internet makes it easy for people to find such information. They are doing so. People's attitudes are a product of the cognitively accessible information they possess and the Internet is providing this information for many. Consumption of one-sided information tends to crystallize people's attitudes about issues and politics and as older generations are replaced with younger ones that are more likely to use the Internet as their primary source of information, public opinion will further polarize. As we argue above, this polarization may actually stimulate participation in the political process.

The polarization of politics can create real problems in the process. For instance, this polarization may be reflected by contention and even combative exchange across party lines in Congress. This can make the policymaking process difficult. Polarization can also create an "us versus them" mentality within the public. Such a mentality leads to a lack of unity across the country, and perhaps violence by those who lose the election and no longer accept that their ideas and beliefs are being represented. People may see the country as an amalgamation of red and blue states as opposed to a union of citizens. Yet, the unlikely positive implication is the motivation that people with strongly held beliefs will have the desire to engage and participate in the system. Polarization can stimulate participation which could result in a more representative democracy, if also a more unsettled and unhappy population.

Clearly more work needs to be done to explore the normative implications of the disruption of the two-sided information flow. The effects of education and civic attentiveness are mixed and may prove significant over time. In addition, more empirical work needs to be done. The relationship between the consumption of one-sided information via the Internet and attitudes about specific political issues needs to be tested. Also, the population replacement argument that we make here could be further substantiated as more data across time become available. For now, the initial look here suggests that the Internet clearly has implications for how people obtain and process information and what this means for political behavior.

7

Click and Donate

The Return of the Small Donor to Campaigns

The role of money and campaign contributions in the United States has been the source of significant debate. The underlying question has been how elected officials can honestly represent their constituents over the moneyed interests whose resources they require to successfully maintain and win a campaign. While this conflict has been a long and tumultuous one, the importance of money for campaigns has grown astronomically as the cost of campaigns has risen significantly based on the need for candidates to purchase access to the mass media, especially time on television (Graber 2006). In this chapter, we propose the Internet allows for a new and different model of fundraising that is less dependent on traditional fundraising networks and ultimately frees candidates from some of the influences that those seeking reform of the finance system have been concerned about for much of the modern era. We focus this analysis on the American experience. While we believe this new type of campaign fundraising has broader implications in other democracies, we concede that different political structures and societies can either vitiate or magnify the effects. Research has suggested that the effectiveness of the Internet as a tool for campaign fundraising can be affected by the nature of the underlying electoral system, making its impact varied across institutional structures or altered by the core attitudes and behavior of voters (Anstead 2008).

The power of the Internet as a fundraiser in American campaigns seems increasingly clear after the most recent electoral cycles, where vast amounts of money were contributed online. Yet, the perception that the Internet would replace or even shift the traditional models of fundraising was not clear or prominently predicted prior to 2008. Early analysis of the trends in online contributions suggested that the Internet could supplement campaign funds and complement traditional outreach programs, but that it was not a paradigm changer (Bimber and Davis 2003). As is true for much of the analysis of the Internet, judgments may have been premature. In the midst of his own online funding success, then-presidential candidate Barack Obama saw something very new occurring around him. In speaking at a traditional fundraiser about his Internet contributions, Obama predicted, "We have created a parallel public financing system where the American people decide if they want to support a campaign, [and then] they can get on the Internet and finance it. And they will have as much access and influence over the course and direction of our campaign [as] has traditionally [been] reserved for the wealthy and the powerful" (Barnes 2008). While there is some hyperbole in Obama's claims, the old paradigm of fundraising based on established political networks needs to be re-evaluated, as millions of dollars flow to candidates through the Internet.

CAMPAIGNS, CORRUPTION, AND CYBERSPACE

The rise of the Internet did not begin the disputes over how campaigns are funded. Money in campaigns is one of the central ideological disputes in the modern electoral era. The primary parties to the argument fall into two camps: those seeking a restriction of the money allowed to be raised by candidates, and those favoring unlimited donations to candidates. The underlying argument concerns the influence of money on either speech or good governance. Those favoring restrictions on the regulation of money in campaigns argue that large sums of money are corrupting to politicians and institutions. More directly, they contend that money distorts representation, weakens democratic ideals, warps political discourse, discourages participation, and ultimately creates a model of electoral participation that is unequal and an electoral competition that is unfair.

The alternative view is framed in terms of the freedom of speech guarantee in the First Amendment to the United States Constitution. The argument can be summarized directly. The defense against tyranny and corruption in the state is vested in the people's ability to speak in opposition to the state. Money is the means by which people can make their speech heard. A restriction on money in the political system is a proverbial gag on speech and is ultimately a threat to democracy. Sometimes this defense-of-speech argument is grounded in the writings of James Madison or John Locke (Samples 2006).

In this chapter, we argue that the baseline dispute between these two sides may no longer be relevant in the Internet age. The increasing use of the Internet in campaigning has begun to transform some of the foundational ways that politics have historically been conducted. As noted earlier, a significant Internet effort has become critical to an effective campaign (Bimber and Davis 2003; Selnow 1998). Candidates are using the Internet to bypass traditional campaign methods to reach voters as well as to raise campaign funds. In previous chapters we have discussed how the Internet has changed various aspects of the political discourse, which can and will affect outcomes and policy. In this chapter, we return to a more direct means by which the Internet can alter how candidates campaign and win. We focus on money in campaigns. Yet, before we reach the Internet itself, we will explore the nature of the underlying campaign system and why it is subject to such a stark and significant change in the Internet era.

Much of the initial motivation for campaign finance legislation was driven by a desire to curtail the spoils system which affected the politics of the post–Civil War era. The Pendleton Act of 1883 attempted to make merit the reason for hiring civil servants rather than political assessments levied on the workers (Hohenstein 2007). Coerced campaign contributions were determined to be corruptive and a more neutral bureaucracy was ultimately desired, though this practice of docking federal employees was widespread. The Republican National Committee assessed all federal employees 1 percent of their salaries in 1878 to support campaign activities (Hohenstein 2007). Though the assessment practice was curtailed, at least openly, little meaningful legislation for the reformation of campaign finance was implemented until the 1970s. There were several laws passed prior to the 1970s regarding disclosure of contributors and the filing of reports, but little was enforced (Mutch 1988).

Serious attempts at campaign finance reform arrived with the passage of the Federal Election Campaign Act (FECA) in 1971. This was followed up by a more comprehensive and definitive statute in 1974 which set forth actual limitations on campaign contributions and strict rules on fundraising (Williams and Tedesco 2006). There was little initial opposition legislatively or politically to the reform, but the U.S. Supreme Court ultimately struck down portions of the bill that unduly restricted free speech in the landmark 1976 case of *Buckley v. Valeo*. Though there was some debate about the need for such legislation, its passage did not satisfy either side in the debate, as it was not restrictive enough for the reformers and too restrictive for the opposition. Further, the rapid growth of interest groups with sources of funding beyond most regulation limited the effectiveness of the legislation (Kobrak 2002). In 2002, the Bipartisan Campaign Reform Act (BCRA) was passed, attempting to fix the earlier legislation primarily by eliminating ways to make unlimited contributions to candidates through party organizations or soft money. The end result again seems to have satisfied few observers.

MONEY, INFLUENCE, AND THE POWER OF SMALL DONORS

The corrupting influence of money in campaigns is an ideologically polarizing notion (Smith 2001). The base allegations are that there is too much money being spent in political campaigns and that money has a corrupting influence. Money buys both votes and elections. The end result is that ordinary citizens are excluded from the political process in favor of moneyed interests that support campaigns. This causes the very pillars of our democracy, which rest on popular representation, to become unsteady and weak. In short, money in campaigns threatens American democracy. The allegations are complex, yet the calculus is much simpler. It is not the money itself that is the most significant fear. It is the compulsion for fundraising that drives concerns of corruption. If candidates need funds to win and special interests or lobbyists supply those funds, then influence is suspected or sometimes presumed. We propose that the Internet may well resolve at least part of this campaign finance quagmire, but before presenting the solutions, we want to be definitive about the nature of the alleged corruption in the campaign finance system used in the United States.

In truth, there is still some question as to whether money represents the corrupting influence alleged. Does it purchase political seats? The research does suggest a correlation between money and electoral success (Alexander 1984). The candidate who raises and spends the most money is more likely to win. This fact is rarely disputed. However, causation is another matter.

A correlation between money and success is not the same as saying money causes success. While a poorly funded candidate is more likely to lose, the explanation could well be that the candidate is unpopular, and so can neither raise money nor collect votes. Further, donors do tend to be rational actors. Donors may attempt to donate to the party or candidate they perceive as most likely to win (Moussalli 1990). These donors are attempting to influence the eventual winner rather than picking the winner. In that case, we have actually reversed the causation relationship. Success brings contributions rather than contributions bringing electoral victory. Because of this causation issue, the more fundamental questions can be neglected. Does it matter? Do the donations influence the behavior of candidates in office?

The debate over the influence of campaign donations is not likely to find resolution. Though overt coercive activity, such as political assessments, no longer exists, the underlying calculus is still valid and operative. The spoils system, of parsing out political positions to contributors and donors, or implementing policy or allocating funds to aid donors, is still quite extant. The primary difference is that politicians are more adept at avoiding evidence of any quid pro quo associated with their actions. During the debate over BCRA, one of the bill's sponsors, Senator John McCain, made the allegation that excess campaign funds were corrupting. Senator Mitch McConnell challenged the allegations concerning congressional spending that favored contributors and called for McCain to name offending senators. McCain would not, or could not (Hohenstein 2007).

As Senator McConnell pointed out above, proving corruption is far different from alleging it. While someone may donate money, the political actor does not necessarily operate in the donor's favor. Scholars studying contributions and policy have found that contributions are often far less important than ideology, party, or constituents in deciding votes (Sabato 1987; Sorauf 1988; Malbin 1984; Grenzke 1989; Welch 1982). Whether this is because contributions matter much less than is perceived, or because scholars have a great deal of difficulty obtaining measures of actual corruption, is debatable. Certainly there are grounds to believe the basic measures are flawed or at best incomplete in their analysis of how office holders juggle competing interests (Lowenstein 1989).

Nonetheless, there is clarity about some facets of this process. Money is important, and certain groups and industries are important sources for these funds. In the traditional campaign, especially costly national campaigns, the candidate will need to go to these donors to raise sufficient funds to reach voters. In the U.S. House of Representatives, where elections are more frequent, fundraising is even more vital (King 1997). Even in the U.S. Senate, which is buffered by six-year terms, senators must raise large sums of money on an almost weekly basis to remain competitive in upcoming elections (Kobrak 2002). Much of this money is raised from a fairly small group of influential donors, using access to the politician as the draw for the donation. Some politicians are better than others. Former president Bill Clinton was adept at using meetings over coffee as an effective means to gather funds from well-heeled contributors. The average citizen has no similar way to gain such access and push their agenda or concerns to the politician in question. In an interview on the television program *60 Minutes* in September 2008, Senator McCain conceded as much and suggested the declining economic condition in the United States was the product of this system. He asserted, "It's been broken by greed and access, aided and abetted by a government in Washington that's dominated by special interests and corruption."

The Internet cannot answer all of the concerns about campaign finance, but it may vitiate the primary concern of influence. Much of the battle over campaign finance continues to be a concern about moneyed interests exerting too much influence at the expense of the average citizen. This is and was possible for two primary reasons. Large donors are necessary to raise the increasingly large amounts of money necessary for national campaigns. Second, large donor recruitment makes the most efficient use of a politician's limited resources, especially time. If politicians are able to raise $10,000 from one telephone call, that allows them to use their remaining time on other campaign activities or even to govern. While a large group of small donors can provide similar funding, the investment in time, effort, and organization makes the attempt almost self-defeating. The costs in staffing an organization for a small donor appeal require resources to be expended, which may ultimately cost more than the funds raised. Gathering a smaller group of wealthy patrons over coffee or dinner is far more efficient and cost-effective.

The Internet changes this calculation on a massive scale. It enables efficiency in raising money from small donors in large amounts with much smaller investments in either organization or staffing. In the most basic sense, it evens the playing field by allowing candidates to compete and raise money outside the traditional venues and networks. Media analysts have already noted the growth of small contributions and its rising importance, terming it "small dollar democracy" (Bonin 2007; Helman 2007). It allows candidates to be less reliant on bundlers and activists for the resources necessary to win. While the amount of money increases, the candidate becomes less beholden to any particular source. The Internet brings the average citizen back into the fundraising equation, and while it will not maximize any particular voice, its ability to reach beyond the more familiar power brokers allows candidates to focus less on the formerly dominant contributors.

This outreach can be accomplished with far fewer resources than it would take to physically canvass a geographic area seeking contributors. This small donor–based fundraising will ultimately shift the very foundation of influence peddling through campaign contributions as candidates begin to grasp the possible alternatives. What makes Internet fundraising significant is it accomplishes the primary goal of those seeking to fund campaigns through the government. It removes the power of any particular interest to unduly influence the candidate by minimizing the importance of any singular contributor. Large sums of money are not attributable to a specific interest or donor, but rather to masses of donors with no particular ability to wield influence as a unified actor. More directly, large numbers of small donors operate as a counterweight to traditional networks of interests and activists.

The power of the Internet as a means to reach small donors has been growing with each election cycle. In 1998, the initial uses of online campaigning showed promise, but simple things like links between candidates' pages and the party were missing (Dulio, Goff, and Thurber 1999). By the 2000 presidential primaries, the effectiveness of the Internet as a fundraising vehicle became apparent. Senator Bill Bradley used the Internet to raise over a million dollars in his upset bid to claim the Democratic nomination from then–vice president Al Gore (Bimber and Davis 2003). In 2000 on the Republican side, Senator McCain was able to raise large funds over the Internet, which helped him remain competitive for far longer than expected with the financially stronger George W. Bush campaign, which had already assembled most of the Republican fundraising strength. McCain repeatedly advertised his webpage, especially after his unexpected, but well-publicized, upset victory over Bush in the New Hampshire Republican primary. He used the Internet to turn his unexpected victory in New Hampshire into an online fundraising juggernaut, raising a then-unprecedented $4 million over the Internet (Salant 2000). In the end, McCain raised $6.4 million from small donors over the Internet (Davis 2003).

The impact on fundraising has become increasingly significant and allows candidates to tap funds to which they may not have had access prior to the Internet (Browning 2002). In the 2004 Democratic presidential primaries, Howard Dean successfully fueled his campaign by using the Internet for both the penetration of the campaign and in raising funds (Trippi 2004). Dean took full advantage of the Internet for fundraising. He collected over $20 million from online contributions. This was a big surprise for most observers, including Dean, who predicted he would be dead last in fundraising during the campaign (Teachout and Streeter 2007). Dean was particularly effective in reaching small donors. This was especially true for young voters, who overwhelmingly gave online rather than through the more traditional avenues (Graf et al. 2006). As chairman of the Democratic Party, Dean also focused on raising funds in small amounts over the Internet rather than focusing more exclusively on large wealthy donors, mimicking the strategy that proved successful for him in his own campaign (Bolton 2005).

In the 2008 campaign, Obama maximized the potential of the Internet to raise unprecedented levels of money. The underlying strategy was still the same: simply networking to assemble people to contribute and encourage others to contribute. Yet, the ability to do this over the Internet generated a vast network that continued to grow through the campaign. A traditional network consists largely of activists, party faithful, lobbyists, and interest groups. Obama's Internet network was far broader, reaching well beyond the party base to virtually anyone with an Internet connection and some interest in the campaign. Contributions could be made with the donor never having spoken to or been enticed by anything other than the webpage and other Internet resources. The webpage itself generated traffic from multiple sources, including the traditional media and social networking websites such as Twitter, Facebook, and MySpace. Vast sums poured into the Obama campaign with no coffees or fundraising dinners required.

Several strategies used by Obama and subsequently the other candidates made online fundraising particularly effective. Initially, the entry donation amounts were very low. Contributors could donate as little as ten dollars, and many did. Though he did raise significant money from larger donations, Obama raised approximately half of his money from people donating $200 or less (Isikoff 2008). Small donors do not require or demand access to the candidate. In the end, the Obama campaign had three million donors. They made 6.5 million donations online totaling more than $500 million. Six million of the 6.5 million donations were made in increments of $100 or less. The average online donation was $80, though the average Obama donor gave more than once (Vargas 2008). Despite the relatively small average amounts donated, the totals were remarkable. In September 2008, Obama's online contributions totaled approximately $100 million dollars. The new calculus for Obama's campaign was that small donations made at a steady rate generate unprecedented amounts of money. Further, particular events drew people to the website to donate. Alaska governor Sarah Palin's acceptance speech was thought to be very effective at the Republican National Convention. It was also effective for Obama, who raised $10 million in the twenty-four hours that followed the speech in online contributions (Vargas 2008).

Aside from allowing small contributions, the Obama campaign successfully presented its appeal and networked its website with popular online addresses. Part of what made the fundraising effort so effective was the campaign's relentless presentation of the donation option to the online community. Early studies of online contributions showed that many people, especially small donors, would contribute without being asked (Graf et al. 2006). The Obama campaign showed that relentless asking works even better. The donation button was prominently displayed on the campaign index page of the website so every visitor would see it. It was placed on social networking websites, e-mails, and in text messaging. The website even added a Web 2.0 innovation by allowing users to customize an e-mail to their friends encouraging them to donate as well. The campaign was able to maximize this contribution appeal though several online communities. Facebook had multiple groups to support the Obama campaign, including 3.2 million supporters in a group called Students for Barack Obama (Vargas 2008). Using these online resources, Obama's campaign was able to assemble an e-mail list containing approximately thirteen million addresses. Using these addresses, the Obama campaign regularly targeted the people on the list with e-mails specifically designed to their level of donation (Vargas 2008). By the conclusion of the campaign, over one billion e-mails were sent.

While the Obama campaign illustrates how the Internet can be effective on the largest stage when raising funds, that is only part of the story. Raising campaign funds on the Internet can be successful, even for outside candidates with little popular recognition outside specific groups. Congressman Ron Paul's campaign for the Republican presidential nomination in 2008 successfully marketed itself on the Internet, generating large sums of money during the primary season. Paul, who always remained a marginal candidate in the polls, raised funds similar to top-tier candidates and sometimes even surpassed them. Paul's supporters helped him raise a then-record $3.4 million online in a single day, and his funding totals regularly outpaced candidates with higher positions in the polls (Vargas 2008). Paul's online success was not driven by large popularity in the general population, but by the ability of the Internet to coordinate interested people from across the nation and induce them to support the campaign financially. The ability of Paul to compete so effectively in fundraising rejects the initial contention that the Internet complements traditional methods and largely favors leading candidates (Bimber and Davis 2003). Further, it allows candidates who would in normal circumstances have been forced to abandon the campaign to continue to compete long after they have exhausted the customary sources of campaign money.

The unforeseen success in Internet fundraising of candidates such as Ron Paul and Howard Dean suggests that future campaigns may become more unpredictable in their scope or outcome. Neither candidate entered the race with the intention of using the Internet campaign to equalize against better-funded and better-known candidates (Teachout and Streeter 2007). Yet, each adapted and became the recipient of a significant surge through the Internet. Online support pushed Dean from a largely unknown and underfunded small-state governor to the status of frontrunner for the Democratic nomination by the beginning of the primary season in 2004. Similarly, Internet funding allowed Paul to continue to campaign against eventual winner John McCain in the 2008 Republican primary when other candidates were no longer raising sufficient funds to compete. Both candidates were able to support their campaign, at least initially, without the usual sources and networks of campaign contributions. Web campaigning has grown with every elections cycle (Foot and Schneider 2006). As more candidates are successful in harnessing the Internet as a source of campaign resources, the ability of the traditional power brokers in the party organization to dictate policy and influence candidates will likely be reduced.

CONCLUSION

The future of fundraising in political campaigns in the United States continues to evolve. The lessons of the past few election cycles illustrate that how money is raised and the amounts of money raised are changing because of the Internet. At first blush, the Internet appears to be increasing the problem of money in politics. Candidates, led by the unprecedented fundraising success of Barack Obama, are raising huge sums over the Internet and increasing the need for competing candidates to raise similar amounts to compete. Yet, much of the evil perceived in campaign donations is not in the money itself, but rather the access and influence it buys. Prior to the Internet, the vast majority of that money was raised from activists, lobbyists, and organized interests. The Internet changes the underlying paradigm of fundraising. It allows candidates to reach far more people and to use small donations to gather even greater sums of money.

The rise of Internet fundraising does not remove traditional fundraising networks or prevent politicians from seeking funds from those networks along with the Internet. We expect that the traditional networks will continue for the foreseeable future for a few reasons. Initially, the present generation of politicians is familiar with, and is largely a product of, this funding system. Second, all money is important and no resource, even an offline resource, will be ignored. Third, donors, lobbyists, activists, and interest groups still have a vested interest in influencing policy and will continue to use their resources to do so. Yet, even if those networks continue as a source of funding, their importance will decline. Politicians increasingly will have the ability to choose from what sources they wish to access. Traditional networks will lose their place as a mandatory component of the campaign. More directly, a candidate need not feel pressured or influenced by any one source as all money is fungible and any one source is not critical. Further, many of the funds that these networks provide will be accessible through the Internet in a way that will bypass the gatekeeper function of the networks. This should accelerate in future years as increasing numbers of candidates are successful outside the traditional network system.

In the end, the larger amounts of money generate a counterintuitive, but clear, result. No particular contribution is vital, so no one group can exercise definitive influence over a candidate who has raised significant funds through a large number of small donations. Even bundlers and networks of donors would be hard-pressed to compete with the potential reach of the Internet with voters and potential donors. This does not mean that interests will not attempt to organize on the Internet to remain a broker for donations by creating lists of potential donors, but gate-keeping on the Internet is difficult at best. The Internet may be able to accomplish what reformers of the campaign finance system have been seeking without any of the alleged deprivations to free speech feared by the opposition (Smith 2006; Hohenstein 2007; Samples 2006). Instead of reducing money, the Internet has multiplied the sources of money and as a result reduced any one source's influence. The Internet has changed the face of fundraising, and savvy candidates will harness that potential with increasing efficiency in future elections.

Finally, it is worth noting that the implications of Internet fundraising are subject to change based on the rules governing campaigning (Anstead 2008). One reason the Internet has risen to greater importance is the lack of substantial controls for online fundraising. Aside from reporting requirements, the Internet is an almost limitless resource and comparatively easier to access than the more traditional sources of funds. However, that might not always be true. The U.S. Supreme Court has begun to remove restrictions on the contributions of artificial constructs such as corporations, allowing them to have an increasingly larger role. In *Citizens United v. Federal Election Commission* (2010), the court overruled previous precedent upholding restrictions on corporate spending to support or oppose political candidates. If corporations are able to funnel limitless contributions to candidates, one could imagine that the Internet may well become irrelevant for fundraising, dwarfed by unregulated corporate contributions. We disagree. In the less regulated campaign environment, the Internet may well be the only source of campaign funds that is independent of larger interests. The Internet may be the lone way for candidates to compete without seeking corporate support.

Is Anyone Listening?

The Online Campaign

Online campaigning has exploded in the United States. With only a few exceptions, virtually every national candidate, and many state or local candidates, have launched some type of campaign presence on the Internet. Some efforts are more sophisticated than others. Some politicians use their webpage as an electronic billboard. Others use it as a portal for supporters to interact, organize, and donate money to the campaign. This expansion of online campaigning has progressed at a rapid rate, and the implications of this expansion are unclear. In this chapter, we explore the growing use of the Internet to campaign and win elections in the United States. Initially, we will review the historic assumptions and motivations behind the use of the Internet to campaign. We will analyze the expectations for online campaigning and compare the competing theories regarding the impact of such campaigning. Finally, we use election data from the 2006 midterm congressional elections and webpage ranking data from the leading web-based ranking service to assess the impact of Internet campaigning. This chapter is, perhaps, the clearest exemplar of the point we are making throughout the book. While there is a wealth of research that claims Internet communication is consequential to election outcomes, there is a dearth of empirical evidence to support the claim. That evidence is provided here.

POLITICS, CAMPAIGNING, AND THE INTERNET: LOOKING BACK

Predicting the nature of the impact of new technology such as the Internet on American politics and the campaign system is difficult, though scholars have tried, typically in broad strokes and mostly with a positive normative view of technology (e.g., Brennan and Johnson 2004; Browning 2002; Davis 1999; Selnow 1998). Early works have explored the influence of the Internet on news gathering, lobbying, campaigning, and even participation (Davis 1999), with much of this research concluding that it has a measurable effect, if not agreeing on the nature or importance of that influence. When confined to discussions of American politics and government, the assertions by scholars are largely affirmative in concluding that there is some impact, though they are not in accord with the magnitude of this impact. The nature of that impact as projected into future political contests is less clear, with differing studies and conclusions on the ultimate significance of the Internet and online campaigning.

The history of the Internet as a political medium in the campaign is not a long one. The 1992 presidential election was the first major national campaign in the United States to make a significant use of the Internet. While there were no web browsers, the Clinton/Gore campaign made use of e-mail, bulletin boards, and discussion groups to disseminate position papers and information on the campaign. The discussion group "alt.politics.Clinton" received approximately eight hundred postings a day during the height of the campaign (Smith 1994). Enthusiastic Clinton volunteers monitored the discussion lists and sent summaries to the campaign offices in Little Rock, Arkansas. This practice was discontinued, however, when the Clinton campaign appeared to ignore the summaries and failed to respond (Smith 1994).

Initially, the Internet remained a fairly low-resource campaign tool, though an early warning of the potential impact of the Internet was displayed in 1994, when then–House Speaker Thomas Foley was defeated in part through the efforts of a political action committee that was organized almost entirely on the Internet (Browning 2002). Since then, the Internet has been growing in importance with each national election cycle. Republican presidential candidate Robert Dole made history in 1996 by being the first political candidate to mention a campaign website at a presidential debate, though he inadvertently failed to give the proper web address (Klotz 2004). Even though Dole misstated the web address, many viewers were able to figure out the correct one and proceeded to collapse the campaign website with the volume of Internet traffic (Klotz 2004). Despite this misstep, a web presence would become an increasing part of any subsequent national campaign. This has held true despite the lack of initial clarity concerning the ultimate utility of the Internet for winning elections.

Nonetheless, the increasing use of the Internet in campaigning has begun to transform some of the foundational ways that politics has historically been conducted, leading some scholars to assert that a significant Internet effort has become integrated into an effective campaign (Bimber and Davis 2003; Selnow 1998). Candidates are using the Internet to bypass traditional campaign methods to reach voters as well as to raise campaign funds. As noted in chapter 7, there is little disputing that the Internet has become an effective means for raising campaign funds. The impact on fundraising has become increasingly significant.

Measuring the role of the Internet beyond fundraising presents more challenges. The most effusive voices suggest an almost groundbreaking role for the Internet. While some political scientists have already surmised that the implications of the Internet are substantial and have caused some changes in the manner in which campaigns are conducted (Davis 1999; Saco 2002; Shapiro 1999), one scholar has expanded the implications of the Internet and predicts that the technology itself will not only improve American democracy, but through the communication of ideas and basic rights, it also will help bring democratic government, and ultimately peace, to the world (Allison 2002).

These more positive interpretations of the role of the Internet suggest a reconstruction of the nature of political organization, as the Internet can provide opportunity for groups to access and engage the public despite having limited means (Morris 1999; Chadwick 2006). As a two-way medium, the Internet provides a mechanism to allow supporters and potential contributors to interact more directly with politicians and parties, creating a differing electoral model that moves beyond the traditional hierarchal structure (Morris 1999). There is some evidence that these projections have merit. Using surveys from 1996 and 2000, Thomas Johnson and Barbara Kaye (2003) find that the Internet empowers individuals and increases interest and participation in politics. Politicians and parties are responding to this perceived impact. Parties, candidates, and government agencies are increasingly active online in creating and providing various forms of political information and engagement opportunities, though there is some question as to whether many people are making use of such opportunities, especially outside the United States (Lusoli and Ward 2005).

To counter the more buoyant predictions concerning the Internet, some scholars have suggested the impact of the Internet is not as significant as has been argued. Directly contrary to the research suggesting greater degrees of public interest, David Tewksbury (2003) used weblogs to measure actual Internet usage and finds that more than half of Internet users do not access public affairs information. Studies of the elections conducted in 1996 and 2000 yield less optimistic results as well. Empirical research has suggested that the effects of the Internet in the campaign may in fact be modest and have a limited impact on elections (Bimber 1998; Bimber and Davis 2003).

In 1996, studies found that the magnitude and value of the Internet was less than expected, with the actual numbers of voters using websites fairly small compared to the voting electorate (Davis 1999; Chadwick 2006). Similarly, based on measures in 2000, Bimber and Davis (2003) reviewed the impact of the Internet and ultimately predict that, though the Internet has a role, it is unlikely to play a critical function in future elections. Though clearly an early study, Bimber (2001) found that Internet use does not correlate with voting, suggesting that the medium is of limited use in the campaign. Nonetheless, in reviewing the 2000 election, some scholars did find that the use of the Internet as a structural component in elections could alter some elements of the electorate itself (Gainous and Wagner 2007; Solop 2001). However, this finding is limited to the use of the Internet as an actual means of voting.

Even researchers willing to concede the growth of the Internet as a campaign vehicle argue that its importance may be overstated. Proposing a normalization thesis, these scholars suggest that as politicians and political operatives become more familiar with the technology, they will gain expertise and ultimately package and control the Internet as a medium (Chadwick 2006; Davis 1999; Margolis and Resnick 2000). In the context of an Internet campaign, the wealthier parties or candidates should be able to hire the best web designers and better integrate the web into the larger campaign vehicle (Chadwick 2006). As is the case with traditional campaigning, the groups with resources will be advantaged, and the natural campaign advantages will not shift in any revolutionary ways (Klotz 2004). The normalization thesis suggests, at least to some degree, that the Internet will become significant, if only to be ultimately co-opted.

Outside the United States, studies also reach more limited conclusions. Early research from the 1997 and 1998 campaigns in the United Kingdom conclude that, though candidates make use of the technology, they and the parties are limited in the use of online resources and use the Internet primarily as an electronic newspaper or online brochure with limited interactivity (Ward and Gibson 2003; Gibson and Ward 1998). As in the United States, the use of the Internet as a campaign tool increased in subsequent elections as a means of organization and communication. Nonetheless, the usage by candidates was extremely limited, with only approximately one quarter of the candidates having campaign websites in 2001 (Ward and Gibson 2003). The more limited use of the Internet by the candidates in the United Kingdom is in part driven by campaign laws, and its lower rates of Internet penetration relative to the United States (Chadwick 2006). Interestingly, higher cell phone ownership in the United Kingdom did lead to campaign use of cellular networks and text messaging as a campaign tool (Coleman and Hall 2001).

Ultimately, the Internet appears to have been of limited value in helping voters in the U.K. reach decisions, as it trails both television and newspapers widely in contemporary surveys of media influence (Chadwick 2006). Similar, though admittedly not definitive, conclusions were reached in an examination of European elections. In the 2004 European Parliamentary elections, the data suggest the Internet is a secondary medium (with some variance based on the nation), though it appears increasingly integrated into the larger campaign structure (Lusoli 2005). Particularly in the United Kingdom, only 6 percent of voters reported using the Internet to gather information in the same 2004 election (Lusoli and Ward 2005).

THE INTERNET CAMPAIGN: LOOKING FORWARD

Future projections made based on past data are difficult at best, as the familiarity with the technology by candidates, the penetration of that technology into the electorate, as well as innovations as yet unseen, make the process dynamic. Further, the relevant variables are not only hard to measure, but difficult to ascertain as an ongoing concern. Some well-founded assumptions are already coming into question. Despite the more limited use and effect of the Internet in previous campaigns, there are reasons to believe its importance will grow.

There is little argument that the Internet will force at least some change in political candidates because of the ease in disseminating information and the increased avenues in which to interact and engage with the electorate. Even beyond the easing of communication barriers, the Internet creates its own dynamic for the interaction of politicians with the public. Candidates' websites can and do become venues for policy debate (Stromer-Galley 2000). This creates a new type of campaign problem as candidates can lose control of the issues on their own website. Further, the Internet allows for easy entrance for interest groups and third parties, resulting in literally dozens of "digital" parties in both the United States and the United Kingdom (Norris 2001). Even without a physical presence, these third parties can present a sophisticated image across the Internet despite limited resources (Ward et al. 2003). Additionally, communication need not be one-way, as in the case of advertisements purchased for broadcast television, radio, or the print media, but can be interactive and engage the public through forums and e-mail (Schneider and Foot 2002). As we project these changing dynamics into the future, the Internet may alter electoral structure by changing how we vote, and ultimately, who votes.

While some political scientists have known and predicted for some time that the Internet is likely to be an important element of campaigning and communication for future candidates, empirically measuring that influence has been difficult. As a campaign medium, the Internet presents a new form of interaction with the electorate. Unlike television, there are virtually no inadvertent viewers for a campaign website. Television allows candidates to reach a pool of both interested and uninterested voters, whereas a campaign website or other web campaigning will service only those who seek out the candidate. Instead of seeking the voter, the Internet permits the voter to find the candidate with surprising effect. Internet campaign videos can far outreach traditional advertising, as was the case with the video supporting Barack Obama's 2008 campaign for the Democratic presidential nomination, titled "Yes, We Can!" The video reached nearly four million people in just a few weeks (Memmott and Lawrence 2008). By comparison, Hillary Clinton's competing nationally-televised town hall meeting reached a fraction of that audience despite its high cost (Rich 2008).

While it is not impossible that a person could reach a website through mistyping the web address, the chances are extremely small. Consequently, a website would likely have a lesser reach among the casual and likely undecided voters, especially to those with limited knowledge. Nonetheless, even with that limitation, a website can create a stronger intensity among voters because of the nature and the length of exposure. Television advertisements are typically about thirty seconds in duration. The average visitor to a campaign website will stay for over eight minutes (Klotz 2004). This allows for the candidate to disseminate more information and convey positions on a number of issues, while allowing the visitor to self-select areas of interest, from volunteering to voting records. Studies of participation regularly show better educated and informed voters are more likely voters (Verba, Schlozman, and Brady 1995). As these are also the same voters who are most probable to visit websites, the Internet allows a more forceful and concentrated pitch to the voters most likely to participate.

Beyond simply being likely voters, Internet visitors to campaign websites are persons who have at least some interest in the candidate. This allows information to be targeted to an audience possessing some degree of curiosity with at least some likelihood of being persuaded by an effective campaign pitch. It allows those visitors to the website a dynamic and multifaceted experience with the campaign, including an ability to interact with the candidate through forums and electronic town hall meetings (Klotz 2004). Narrowly tailored websites can target information at specific segments of the population or particular demographics (Coleman and Hall 2001). If done well, a website can be a regular destination for not just information, but also social interaction, supplying the type of satisfaction that might drive larger levels of participation when considered in light of participation models (see Sabatier 1992).

This effect can be magnified by drawing the web user into the larger campaign apparatus. The website can be connected to social networking websites such as MySpace, Facebook, and Twitter, creating a broad sweeping effect that draws interested persons back into range of the campaign message regularly, in ways not possible for traditional campaign methods, including television. Though this type of linking is logical, early research suggests that it is not happening to the degree that one might suspect, and the measuring of the impact of such links is a difficult proposition (Foot et al. 2003). Nonetheless, one might expect that future candidates and campaigns will more successfully integrate such outreach. They may be forced to do so. Studies in the United States and the United Kingdom indicate that large numbers of citizens want to interact and engage with politicians through the Internet and online forums (Coleman and Gotze 2001; Cornfeld, Rainie, and Horrigan 2003). Future candidates may want to adopt the technology, or the technologies may generate their own candidates.

Finally, it is worth noting that the entire Internet campaign can be, and often is, integrated into the more traditional aspects of the campaign. Even when seen through the limited paradigm of the traditional campaign machine, the web campaign can be an important component for success. Candidates use opponents' websites for opposition research for debates, commercials, or even competing websites. While this may not necessarily produce a better candidate, it will likely produce a different type of candidate and a different style and approach to the campaign.

CHANGING THE COST DYNAMIC: INTERNET INFLUENCE ON CAMPAIGNS

Few would argue with the proposition that contemporary politics is very much affected by changing technologies such as the Internet. At a very fundamental level, technology advances are affecting the very way that government goes about its tasks in almost every aspect. From filing taxes to obtaining federal documents, the manner by which the government interacts with people is changing rapidly.[1] These changes are no less important for the evolving nature of political campaigning. Nonetheless, it often is difficult to measure this impact and the importance of the evolving uses of technologies like the Internet in real terms. To address this, we create a theoretical understanding of the effect of the Internet on modern campaigning, and we test this theory using data from the 2006 midterm congressional elections.

Though early formulations of campaigns and participation behavior could not have predicted the substantial technological innovation of the Internet, the basic theory is sound. As we did in chapter 4, we adopt and apply the basic logic of political participation. The Internet presents a dynamic change in campaigning technology, but it does not change the basic calculus behind why people vote and campaign. It simply adds a new procedural lens and some novel variables to the equation. For voters, the choice concerning whether to vote or otherwise participate in politics or campaigns is still driven in part by individual-level costs or economic considerations (Downs 1957; Riker and

Ordeshook 1968, 1973; Tullock 1967; Barry 1970). Limited resources restrict an individual's ability to participate, and therefore help explain the disparity in levels of participation for different socioeconomic groups (Verba et al. 1993).

Not only does learning about candidates and issues present a significant cost for individuals, but explaining such things to large numbers of voters is increasingly costly for the campaign. These costs ultimately curtail the reach of a candidate who can only marshal limited resources. Traditionally, candidates must be selective about both their means and method of campaigning in order to maximize positive turnout. Many potential voters in large campaigns are regularly neglected as candidates attempt to maximize the power of their resources and reach for larger groups at the expense of smaller ones, or more sympathetic groups at the expense of neutral ones. This puts an increasing strain on candidates and campaigns, as modern outreach often involves buying time in the mass media, or more specifically, on television, which has regularly become the medium of choice and is a significant drain on campaign resources (Graber 2006).

The Internet presents a change in this cost dynamic. It allows for easier outreach and education of the voters at a fraction of the cost of traditional media. From both the campaign side and the voter side, the cost is minimized, and the potential exchange is far more substantive as the Internet can hold significantly more information and is interactive in scope. The targeting is improved and at a lower cost. Websites gather information on visitors, allowing sophisticated programs to parse the lists and target populations with campaign material tailored to each person's interest. The initial question presented herein is whether one could affect voting results simply by lowering the cost of information delivery and engaging the electorate using a considerably less costly means, such as the Internet. By accessing voters through the Internet, candidates should be able to provide voters with more information than might otherwise be possible and reach voters that traditional campaign advertising might otherwise miss.

If this style of campaigning on the Internet is effective, the end result is clear. A popular campaign website on the Internet should effectively reach and motivate voters to support a candidate at the polls. This should create a measurable effect. Candidate webpages should be an increasingly important explanatory variable for electoral success as their potential reach and penetration are significant, especially when compared to traditional campaign costs. The effectiveness of using the Internet as a means for distribution will be highly dependent on the penetration the website has in the Internet. This factor, which we will call web presence, allows for significant variability, as even the best-designed websites are electorally insignificant when they are not widely seen and distributed. We concede that there may be some expectation that the overall effect is blunted by the digital divide, or the inability of some Americans to access the Internet (see Mossberger, Tolbert, and Stansbury 2003). As we argued in chapters 4 and 5, the digital divide has implications for political participation. Nonetheless, the implications of the divide are not as significant here. Initially we would note that, even with the digital divide, campaign technology can still move large segments of the population and influence results even if the reach is not comprehensive. Further, any limitation presented by the divide seems a largely temporal restraint in the context of the campaign. As technology gains greater penetration and voters increasingly use the Internet to access information, the significance of the Internet as a campaign tool should continue to grow, even if the impact is more limited in the current environment.

MEASUREMENT AND METHODOLOGY

After some descriptive analyses, we use a pair of two-stage least squares models to estimate the effect of web presence (measured using Google PageRank as described in chapter 2), political experience, incumbency, district and race competitiveness, campaign spending, party affiliation, and chamber of Congress on votes received. We use a two-stage approach here to address the possible endogenous variable. It is possible that a high web presence is actually a result of electoral popularity. Hence, our dependent variable may serve as a proxy for the cause of high web presence. Standard linear regression models assume that errors in the dependent variable are uncorrelated with the independent variables. When this is not the case, linear regression using ordinary least squares (OLS) no longer provides an unbiased model estimate. Two-stage least-squares regression uses instrumental variables that are uncorrelated with the error terms to compute estimated values of the problematic predictors, and then uses those computed values to estimate a linear regression model of the dependent variable. Since the computed values are based on variables that are uncorrelated with the errors, the results of the two-stage model are optimal.

We use web traffic and the race of the candidate to predict web presence and then use those predicted values in the second stage of our estimation. We estimate two separate models, one for Democrats and one for Republicans, to prevent a violation of the independence assumption in linear models. The total votes received by one candidate is negatively correlated with the total votes received by the opponent. Thus, the assumption would be violated if we estimate the relationship using one model. Using OLS, we estimated total votes received as a function of web traffic and candidate race to assure that they were not correlated with total votes received, confirming that they are suitable as predictors in the first stage of our two-stage models. None of these predictors are significant at the 0.05 level in either the Republican or Democrat models.

We measure web traffic using data gathered from Alexa.com. The values represent ranking based on the number of hits. We inverted the rankings because those with less traffic had a higher value representing a lower ranking, making interpretation more intuitive. Some might expect web traffic to be correlated with total votes received if our theory is accurate, but we did not expect it to be, for two reasons. First, hits repeated from the same person would indicate higher traffic. Alternatively, it is reasonable to expect that potential voters may visit each of the major candidate's webpages for a given race. Thus, they would cancel each other out. Nevertheless, it is correlated with web presence (Google PageRank), making it a good predictor in the first stage. Finally, race of the candidate is used for an extra control.

We utilize several control variables in the models as well. Each was selected because the extant literature suggests they are important in explaining candidates' share of the vote. The legislative elections literature suggests that political experience is an important source of electoral success (Abramowitz 1991; Bond, Covington, and Fleisher 1985; Jacobson 1992; Krebs 1998; Squire 1989). Thus, we included two measures of political experience. The first is the number of years holding elected office, and the second is the number of years in Congress. The literature also suggests that incumbency advantages candidates, helping them to garner more votes (Abramowitz 1975; Cox and Morgenstern 1995; Krebs 1998; Levitt and Wolfram 1997; Petrocik and Desposato 2004). So, we also employ a dummy variable for incumbency.[2]

We included the number of candidates in each race because this influences the number of votes garnered by candidates (Holbrook and Tidmarch 1993;

Krebs 1998). In addition, district/state competitiveness helps determine the electoral success of both incumbents and challengers (see Breaux and Gierzynski 1991; Koetzle 1998; Welch and Hibbing 1997). District/state competitiveness was measured by subtracting the total number of votes attained by the loser of the previous election from the total number of votes attained by the winner in each respective district/state. Evidence indicates that campaign spending is a determinant of electoral success (Erikson and Palfrey 1998; Green and Krasno 1988; Jacobson 1990), so we also constructed a measure of campaign spending differential by subtracting the challenger's spending from the incumbent's spending. We then divided this differential by 100,000 to make the estimate easier to interpret. We also included candidates' chamber in the models because those in the Senate will obviously garner more votes, so this allows us to control for such and examine the effect of web presence across chambers.

Finally, the descriptive analysis looks at web presence across states with varying median education levels. We do not include races from all fifty states in this sample because, as we mentioned previously, the analysis examines only competitive 2006 races. For the purpose of this study, states were coded as "lower education states" when the median percentage of those with at least a bachelor's degree was beneath the national median (U.S. Census 2000).

FINDINGS

While the focus of this study is on the effectiveness of Internet campaigning, we also explore the variation in a candidate's web presence. This exploration is useful because it provides a descriptive foundation for understanding the nature of this growing phenomenon. With conflicting literature on where and how we might see differences in the web presence of candidates, we start by looking for variation across some basic categories, including party affiliation, chamber, and region.

Initially, we test some widely held suspicions and assumptions about Internet use in political campaigns in the United States. Democrats in Congress were at the forefront of bringing public attention to the Internet (e.g., Al Gore's High Performance Computing Act of 1991). We might expect that they would have a greater web presence than their Republican counterparts. The data confirm this expectation. As apparent in table 8.1, Democrats have a significantly greater web presence than that of their partisan counterparts.

Next, given that Senate races are generally more visible, it is reasonable to expect that Senate candidates would have a greater web presence than House candidates. Again, this expectation is also confirmed. Finally, in 2000, the Department of Commerce issued a report revealing that Internet access was more prevalent in homes with higher education. Because education levels are typically lower in some states, candidates may not have the same incentive to campaign on the web. Therefore, we might expect the web presence of candidates in those states to be weaker than that of candidates in other states. As can be seen in table 8.1, the data suggest this is not the case. A candidate's web presence is virtually equal across lower and higher education states.

Before moving on to the multiple regression analysis of the effectiveness of Internet campaigning, it is important to note that the bivariate correlation between web presence and total votes received is significant (Pearson's $r = 0.29$, $p < 0.01$). This relationship is clear in figure 8.1. The magnitude of the effect is quite strong. The number of votes received increases by nearly 700,000 votes when moving from the lowest web presence to the highest. This estimate is obviously bolstered by the fact that chamber is not controlled for in this graph. Members of the Senate generally get more votes due to having a larger constituency and they should have larger web presence due to being a higher-profile race, but web presence goes up for the lower total votes too. Thus, it is consistently rising for low-vote and high-vote races. Nonetheless, we do control for chamber in our multivariate models. While the relationship between the

Table 8.1 Web Presence across Categories

	Mean Web Presence	Standard Deviation	P-Value
Democrats	2.07	0.68	
			0.00
Republicans	1.52	0.66	
House	1.69	0.68	
			0.02
Senate	1.96	0.77	
Below Median Education	1.75	0.77	
			0.42
Above Median Education	1.84	0.68	
Number of Cases = 173			

Note: Data come from Google PageRank, http://www.TheGreenPapers.com, and the U.S. Census 2000. P-value represents the probability of being wrong in rejecting the null hypothesis that there is no difference across categories in the general population (T-tests—equal variances assumed).

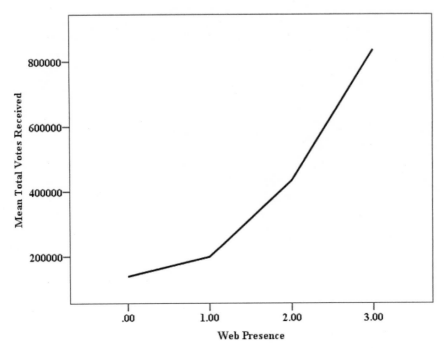

FIGURE 8.1
Votes Received by Candidate Web Presence

Source: Google, Inc., and the Federal Elections Committee; available at www.TheGreenPapers.com.

numbers of votes received and web presence is revealing, it is not conclusive, because this effect may be vitiated when controlling for other factors that influence the number of votes candidates receive. That said, the results reported in table 8.2 indicate that this is not the case, at least for Democrats.

As mentioned above, there is an interesting partisan story to be told here. The effects of both web presence and the control variables tell different tales for Democrats and Republicans in the 2006 election. The most significant difference is that web presence seems to matter for Democrats and not for Republicans, while campaign spending and experience was important for Republicans but not for Democrats. Web presence has a significant bivariate relationship with the total votes received for both Democrats (Pearson's r = 0.25, p = 0.02) and Republicans (Pearson's r = 0.33, p < 0.01), but this relationship dissipates when controlling for other factors in the Republican model. This suggests that the bivariate relationship is spurious for Republicans. A combination of the differences across the models explains the variation between the parties.[3] There are two variables that were significant in the Republican model, but not in the Democrat model: political experience and campaign spending. We estimated three more two-stage models for Republicans to isolate which of these variables explains away the variance that web presence seems to capture in the bivariate model. The results indicate that it is a combination of the two. In the first model, we removed the political experience indicator, and web presence still remained insignificant. In the next, we removed the campaign spending differential, with the same result. Finally, we estimated the model with both removed, and web presence became significant (p = 0.10). This suggests that higher web presence for Republicans is driven by experience and spending, while this is not the case for Democrats.

Overall, this evidence illustrates that the Democratic party's success is due in part to their web efforts. The Democrats' web presence is significantly higher than that of Republicans (refer to table 8.1), reflecting a systematically larger outreach to voters through the use of the Internet. The results of the multivariate analysis indicate that this effort bore fruit. By using a two-stage approach, we took steps in the model to address the possibility that the context of this particular election caused the effect. Our method provides support to the contention that the Democrats' share of the vote is not simply a reflection of their relative popularity at the time. In these data, the increased web presence of the Democrats is a predictor of success. The insignificant findings for the Republican model, combined with the lower web presence of Republicans, suggest the possibility that their electoral fate, or at least the number of votes they got, may have increased with more attention to increasing their web presence. More directly, while their successful campaigns were driven largely by traditional indicators, it is possible that they could have improved their results with a greater focus on the Internet.

The specifics of the models paint an even clearer picture. The Democrat model performs well overall; the R^2 is high (0.84) and diagnostics indicate that multicollinearity is not an issue (see table 8.2). Web presence is a significant predictor of the total number of votes even when controlling for the other variables in the model (p = 0.05). For every one unit increase in web presence, the model estimates that candidates receive roughly 279,000 more votes.[4] Interestingly, the magnitude of the effect does not dissipate from that graphed in figure 8.1 when adding controls. Further, the fact that the statistical significance holds up even when controlling for other theoretical predictors lends considerable support to the contention that web presence matters. The

Table 8.2.   The Influence of Web Presence on Votes Received

	B	S.E.	P-Value
Democratic Model			
Web Presence	279.19	141.21	0.05
Years Holding Elected Office	9.58	8.83	0.28
Years in Congress	−6.98	7.61	0.36
Incumbency	481.74	187.06	0.01
Number of Candidates	−721.67	351.50	0.04
District/State Competitiveness	0.00	0.00	0.00
Campaign Spending Differential	−2.18	1.70	0.20
Chamber	289.74	146.63	0.05
Multiple R^2	0.84		
Number of Cases	86		
Republican Model			
Web Presence	−8.32	141.90	0.95
Years Holding Elected Office	14.77	6.93	0.04
Years in Congress	-2.56	7.19	0.72
Incumbency	-2.79	124.12	0.98
Number of Candidates	453.33	453.33	0.46
District/State Competitiveness	0.00	0.00	0.00
Campaign Spending Differential	3.39	1.32	0.01
Chamber	423.66	134.20	0.00
Multiple R^2	0.79		
Number of Cases	87		

Note: Data come from Google PageRank and Alexa, Federal Elections Committee available at http://www. TheGreenPapers.com, and http://wikipedia.org. Table entries are two-stage least squares estimates, associated standard errors, and the probability of being wrong in rejecting the null hypothesis that there is no effect of the independent variables in the model.

Republican model does not perform as well. The R^2 is lower (0.79) and there are only two significant predictors in the model other than years of political experience and campaign spending differential; they are district competitiveness and chamber. The Democratic model has a total of one more significant variable.

The significance of the controls in the Democratic model strengthens the argument that web presence matters, because web presence significance is independent of these other effects. Because the sample consists of only those races that were competitive, some of the traditional predictors of votes garnered do not matter as much as one might expect. Nonetheless, several variables in the model are significant. The estimate for the effect of the number of candidates in the race suggests that for each additional candidate in the race, each respective candidate will lose roughly 721,000 votes. The coefficient for district competitiveness is also significant, but the magnitude is not as large as the other variables (in both models). For every additional vote separating the winner and loser of the previous election, the number of votes decreased by less than 1,000. Finally, not surprisingly, chamber is significant in both models. The estimate indicates that Democratic senators on average got 289,000 votes more than Democratic members of the House. Similarly, Republican senators received 423,000 more votes than their Republican colleagues in the House. This difference would be larger if the sample were all large states where the difference in voter populations between states and House districts is greater.

CONCLUSION

The political campaign is constantly evolving, and there is little doubt that the Internet will be an important part of the campaign strategy. Scholars are in the early stages of exploring its impact in terms of voting behavior and change. In this chapter, we present one view on how to measure that influence. Based on these data, campaigning on the Internet is of growing importance. With the lower entry cost to the web, we expect the online campaign to continue to grow as a matter of financial expediency, as well as a crafted means of targeting and engaging the electorate. Traditional forms of campaigning, including media advertisements, mass mailings, and traveling to give stump speeches, while often effective, are considerably more costly than creating a web presence. We do not suggest that candidates could forego these more traditional forms of campaigning, but cultivating a web presence as a supplement integrated into the traditional campaign structure would certainly appear to be of benefit, with relatively low cost.

Trying to determine the implications of the Internet as a source of political information and engagement is like trying to hit a moving target, as the number of voters using the medium is still a relatively small, yet clearly growing, part of the electorate. Further, the techniques used are evolving and growing as well. The Internet today, which includes faster transmissions, along with mobile devices that connect to the Internet, is far different from the Internet first measured in many of the studies from just a few years ago. More voters and a new generation of younger voters are moving to the Internet as a significant source of political information. Additional work needs to be done to understand what likely will be one of the more significant changes in politics and voting in the next decade. By no means does this study address every question that needs answering when it comes to this burgeoning subject of inquiry, but it begins to put one type of physical measure on the value of an Internet presence in the campaign.

Nonetheless, we concede there are questions unanswered. The influence of web advertising on individual-level vote choice also needs exploration. In addition, more research needs to be done to investigate variation in the effectiveness of Internet campaigning based on the increasing quality and availability of interactive applications on candidates' webpages. These are difficult measures, as innovations are rapid, research is often far slower, and parties and candidates are not waiting to reach their own conclusions. Considering the fact that nearly every candidate for major public office in the United States now has a webpage, they did not need empirical evidence to believe that it would be effective. Nonetheless, now they have it. In these data, a robust web presence during a political campaign does have a positive impact on the number of votes garnered.

9

Evolution, Revolution, and the Internet Revisited

In lamenting the modern state of the Senate, the late Democratic senator Robert Byrd observed of the legislative chamber, "It is not the Senate that I once knew. The Senate has lost its soul" (Evans 2002: 281). Byrd, a long-serving senator, was observing something that many people already knew. The Senate had changed. Studies have convincingly demonstrated that the chamber is no longer the collegial and gentlemanly place of old (Baker 2002; Sinclair 2001). In the modern Congress, members send digital messages on networks like Twitter lambasting the opposition or commenting on legislation as it is being negotiated. During Barack Obama's first address to a joint session of Congress, representatives and senators were commenting live on the speech using Twitter. Senator Claire McCaskill had to later apologize after her own mother pointed out that it was rude to the president (Marrero 2009).

It is a different and evolving political environment. The instantaneous nature of communication makes for a surprisingly more spontaneous, or perhaps more honest, dialogue, though elected officials are increasingly forced to retract or retreat from these electronic comments. Former House Speaker Newt Gingrich used Twitter to call then–Supreme Court nominee Sonya Sotomayor a racist (Khan and Tapper 2009). Gingrich, a short time later, decided to retract the statement noting that his original reaction, which he had distributed across the nation, was too strong and direct. He added, "The word 'racist' should not have been applied to Judge Sotomayor as a person" (Gingrich 2009). On the Internet, reactions and retractions move at a remarkable pace.

Successful politics involve harnessing new technology. It also means using it to one's advantage rather than as a detriment. As much as some older and more experienced politicians would prefer tried and familiar political discourse and competition, the new age is already here. Looking back at an idealized political system is not only poor strategy, but is also inaccurate. Everything changes, including those American institutions that many hold as works of political genius. A great deal of scholarship rests on finding the perfect moment in time, not just for people, but for institutions (see Cox and McCubbins 1993; Shepsle 1989). To pursue this moment is to forget that institutions, like everything, shift with the era. There is no moment when state institutions operated exactly as designed. In the instant of their creation and adoption, institutions were placed within a larger society where nothing was static, beginning with how the people understood the role and function of government. Governing thus became, and continues to be, a process of adaptation and learning where nothing is fixed and nothing is permanent.

It is in understanding this change that the nature and function of government and politics becomes clearer. In lamenting the state of the Senate, Byrd was really observing an evolution in how the Senate operates and legislates. Though he might see the change as deleterious, there was never any true fixed notion of perfection as to how the Senate should operate. In truth, like all of government and society, the Senate has been changing for some time (Sinclair 1989). Senators from generations preceding Byrd likely would have met his ideal version of the Senate with a rejection similar to the one he held for the 2002 version. New senators use e-mail, webcams, Twitter, Facebook, MySpace, YouTube, and many other new and developing avenues to reach, influence, and listen to constituents. The modern legislature will inevitably be very different from past ones.

In the preceding chapters, we have explored how technology, and specifically the Internet, forces a change in how people engage with the state and how those changes will eventually shift representation and policy. We have explored these changes using several different approaches and measures. We have used measures of voters, students, Internet users, and census data to begin to describe how Americans have embraced this new technology and its penetration into society. We examined how online learning differs from traditional learning and the implications of the diverse yet polarizing medium. We have demonstrated that the operation of the Internet changes how people interact with politicians and state institutions, forcing adaptations in everything from who votes, how we vote, and ultimately, how we understand and participate with the political system. As highlighted throughout the book, we are not the first to explore these topics. The real contributions here are theoretical approaches to understanding the role of the Internet in politics and empirical tests that seek to hold our theories and existing theories to a measurable and more reliable standard. In doing so, we hope to provide generalizable results for others to consider and compare. While clearly this book is not the end of attempts to understand and measure the impact of the Internet on politics, it is among the first literature in the field to step beyond assumption and conjecture to look at actual measures in multiple areas. We hope to be among a growing literature that moves away from personal observation combined with individualized predictions.

In this concluding chapter, we will sum up the major patterns that emerge over time and consider the implications of this type of change for the future of the American system. We conclude with thoughts on the broader implications of Internet as an increasingly integral part of our society and lives.

THE LESSON FROM TELEVISION

The Internet is not the first major technological advance in communication technology to cause political evolution. Everything from newspapers to radio has had an impact. Advances in technology continue to be important exogenous stimuli on society because they alter the way people interact with the state. In this book, we have attempted to demonstrate that though shifting ideas are often a powerful stimulus for change, environmental and operational shifts can be just as important. Technology only can revolutionize a system or state by creating alternate ways for the people to engage state institutions. As we have shown in this book, the implications can be significant. It can change how people interact, or how they work, or even how they vote. This substantive change in people or society can then affect how state institutions operate. If there is a change in communication, it might affect how people evaluate political information or how they see and understand politicians or political candidates. This can alter how society engages with institutions. It may lead to the ascendance of a political group or demographic group that is well situated to adapt and take advantage of the technological stimuli. If the control of a state institution changes, then public policy will change as well, with society then having to alter itself to adjust and react to the new policies. While it might at first seem that the impact of a new technology such as the Internet is largely an issue of efficiency, the evidence suggests something far more significant. Technological advancement is forcing adaptation, evolution, and in some cases, revolution.

Predicting the scope and effect of the Internet is a difficult task, though the impact of television provides some baseline to understand how revolutionary technology can be, not only in the social sphere, but in how politics and a political system operate. The pervasiveness of television in the home transforms not only how people get the news, but the kind of news, and ultimately the kind of candidates who are successful (Graber 2006). Because television allows voters to see and hear the candidate in their living rooms, it has reduced the importance of party labels, at least in highly visible elections. Abraham Lincoln or Harry Truman might have suffered in the television age because of appearance or on-air demeanor. Ronald Reagan, meanwhile, might not have been nearly as successful in his campaigns if not for his familiarity with, and comfort in front of, the camera.

Assessing technological influences on politics is never easy. The implications of television have been subject to a larger debate. Some have argued that television has so trivialized politics that its impact will be substantively destructive to the political system (Postman 1985). Depending on which line of reasoning one follows, the effect of television is destructive to social organization (Putnam 2000), or it is a key component of a more informed and engaged society (Gould 1946; Graber 2006). Television has changed how candidates are covered and has a significant impact on the success or failure of a candidate (Graber 2006). In 1996, Ross Perot ran a presidential campaign almost entirely through the use of television appearances and paid advertisements. The power of television has led to some foundational beliefs about politics. Because of the importance of television coverage, many campaigns are controlled by the amount of money that can be raised in order to increase visibility on television. Congresspersons regularly give speeches to largely empty chambers for television consumption. The president maximizes his power through public appeals based on media access and television (Kernell 1997).

As we have argued throughout this book, the Internet strikes at some of the pillars of television-based politics and will ultimately transform the television-dominated campaign process. While there is no evidence that the Internet will replace television in the immediate future, it can be a means to bypass television as a less-expensive way to reach voters, donors, and activists. Howard Dean's early success in the 2004 Democratic presidential primaries was based on the use of the Internet and not television (Trippi 2004). Eventual primary winner John Kerry followed the lead of Dean and ultimately ended up raising nearly a third of his campaign funds through the Internet (Graber 2006). Barack Obama revolutionized campaign funding by drawing tens of millions of dollars from small donors through his website (Vargas 2008). Television has become a way to redirect people to the web where fundraising, advocacy, and communication are more interactive and engaging. Candidates use television to give out web addresses where everything from policy details to campaign plans may be posted and updated.

The Internet also provides a means to bypass the gate-keeping function of the media and reach interactively to voters. Candidates do not simply use the Internet as a complementary form of campaigning; they use it to avoid the media entirely and make announcements such as a choice of running mate or where to meet. E-mail has replaced press conferences as the easiest way to disseminate information on the campaign. Barack Obama not only sent targeted and repeated e-mails, but complemented the approach with text messaging announcements. Even before Obama's campaign, e-mail had become a prominent campaign tool. It was estimated more than a billion messages were sent to voters urging them to support a particular candidate in 2004 (Graber 2006). As a political venue, the Internet allows candidates to control some of their own message and avoid the gate-keeping function that the media play between candidates, government, and the people.

Further, the Internet strikes at the very cost model that governs politics. The cost of being online is comparatively small when compared to traditional campaign outreach, which requires expensive printing costs or paid staffers. The Internet permits continual outreach with electronic communications that are almost cost-free in comparison. This is complemented by a participatory environment, ranging from individual bloggers to large organized interests such as Moveon.org. A well-executed Internet campaign can be better

targeted and more interactive than the traditional television-dominated strategies of previous elections, and it requires a fraction of the funds. As we analyzed in chapters 7 and 8, the effectiveness of the Internet in fundraising and
campaigning may radically alter the environment. The ability to raise large
sums of money from a vast network of small donors reduces the influence of
traditional political networks. Further, despite some initial conclusions that
the Internet's influence on outcomes was peripheral, we have demonstrated
that successful Internet campaigns predict success at the ballot box.

THE DIGITAL DIVIDE AND THE FUTURE OF INTERNET POLITICS

The Internet is still a very young technology. Its application in the political
and electoral sphere is even younger, with the adoption of Internet strategies having only occurred in the last decade. Where the Internet likely will
diverge in comparison to television is in the interactive nature of the new
medium. While television was revolutionary in the way that it transformed
how information is delivered, the Internet serves as a means of two-way communication. The Internet allows for participation in a way television does not.
This is particularly important to the study of politics, as campaigns and communications can be maximized with the interactive character of the Internet
(Allison 2002; Nussbaum 2004; Shapiro 1999; Trippi 2004; Wilhelm 2000).
In truth, the Internet may well swallow television by delivering video content
over high-speed connections in a far more user-friendly fashion. The Internet
user can decide when, what, and how much of anything to watch, while the
television viewer is at the mercy of the broadcaster. With Web 2.0 innovations
allowing the user to customize their own experience, it may not be long before
scheduled television from broadcast stations becomes a very antiquated and
declining means to deliver video content.

The import of these changes is hard to measure, but the implications are
likely significant. Scholars already have studied how factors ranging from
income, education, race, age, gender, and attitude affect participation in politics (Abramson 1983; Campbell et al. 1960; Conway 1991; Rosenstone and
Hansen 1993; Verba, Schlozman, and Brady 1995; Wolfinger and Rosenstone
1980). Technology provides a new way to understand how these factors may
affect participation by easing access for some and not for others. The early
data, consistent with the findings above, suggest that technology, because
of uneven distribution, continues to maximize the inequity of participation

along racial and socioeconomic lines (Allison 2002; Alvarez and Nagler 2001; Department of Commerce 2002; Mossberger, Tolbert, and Stansbury 2003). While it is not clear how technology will affect things such as voting behavior in the long term as the penetration of such technology increases, it is currently evident that those with higher education and income are not only more likely to participate in politics online, but they are also more likely to have an interest or desire to use Internet resources for political purposes (Mossberger, Tolbert, and Stansbury 2003). The digital divide has, in some ways, become a form of democratic divide, but only for now. The way that the Internet grows and penetrates society may magnify or perhaps reduce this divide.

There clearly are temporal limitations to any measure of the impact of this new technology. Our measures are limited to a point in time because the penetration, or even the rate of penetration, of Internet technology or other advance technology is not fixed or static. It will change, and with it the implications of its use will change as well. The degree that people or politicians can predict the usefulness of technology is uncertain. It was not until 1956 that television was available in 75 percent of homes, and the impact of television on the nature of social organization is still being analyzed and debated (Gould 1946; McBride 1998; Postman 1985; Putnam 1995a, 2000). In contrast, Internet adoption has been fairly rapid. Today, a majority of Americans are online in some fashion. They are doing everything from downloading music to bidding in auctions, posting political commentaries, or rallying for political candidates (Trippi 2004). For those who can anticipate correctly, as Barack Obama did in the 2008 presidential election, the benefits of technology can be significant in both the penetration of the message and in the generation of campaign financing and campaign workers.

The importance of the digital divide in American politics will depend on several factors going forward. One hopeful sign is the decreasing cost of computers (Saco 2002). Yet, expansion of Internet use is not only dependent on the affordability of home computers, but on the adoption of technology in industry. While it is true that certain disadvantaged populations lack access at their homes, it may be that Internet access will be widely available in the workplace, though the evidence of such access is still limited. Trends in Internet use show that there is an increase in Internet use in the workplace for commercial activities (Department of Commerce 2002). In 1997, only 18 percent of people used the Internet in the workplace. By 2001, the use of the Internet in the workplace had increased to 42 percent (Department of Commerce 2002). Even in these numbers, though, there is some evidence of a digital divide. Managerial and professional occupations disproportionately provide Internet access, with more than two-thirds having used the Internet at work (Department of Commerce 2002). The use of the Internet by individuals working in traditional blue-collar occupations trails significantly, mirroring the access issues at home.

Further, and notwithstanding the increasing work access of the population of Internet users, 80 percent access the Internet from home while only 36 percent use work access. This home dominance is a long-standing pattern in Internet use since the inception of the World Wide Web (Klotz 2004). While it is possible for there to be a sea change in the type of Internet use with an increasing focus on Internet in the workplace, the evidence for such a move is not yet apparent. Home use continues to be the dominant form of Internet access. Nonetheless, there is strong growth in multiple access use, or users who access the Internet from many different locations. This includes users at the workplace (Klotz 2004). This likely will drive computer training in public schools, and ultimately aid the penetration of Internet use into disadvantaged populations, though clearly at a lesser pace. In addition, the use of handheld devices such as smartphones, MP3 players, or even tablet computers like the iPad to access the Internet is presenting new and increasingly affordable means to go online and participate. It is not uncommon for individuals to now be constantly online through portable devices, making the Internet increasingly relevant to their day.

While the pattern of Internet usage may change with increased access through portable devices and at places such as work and public facilities like local libraries and public schools, the present evidence suggests the implications of the digital divide will persist for the immediate future. While 68 percent of Americans now use the Internet, Americans with less education, the elderly, and African Americans continue to lag in Internet use (Fox 2005). Education continues to be a leading indicator of Internet use. Only 29 percent of Americans who have not completed high school have access compared to 89 percent of college graduates (Fox 2005: 2). There is reason to be concerned about the reach of the Internet to these groups. Data suggest that this might be a persistent pattern. The number of new Internet users has declined from 2002, where more than 17 percent of users were in their first year of Internet use. In addition, the number of Americans who have never used the Internet or even e-mail has remained static over the last few years. Twenty-two percent of Americans were non-users in 2002. In 2005, the number of non-users was roughly the same at 23 percent (Fox 2005). While no one can predict the future with any true degree of certainty, the evidence clearly suggests that the digital divide, while not as large and encompassing as it once was, clearly still exists and will continue to be important in many areas, including political participation, for some time. There is support for the notion that the divisions based on technology will be temporal (Saco 2002), but they could persist for some time.

There is no reason to believe that the data presented here, along with the findings of other scholars, represent any fixed or permanent understanding of how technology will continue to structure or influence politics in future decades. In fact, the only certain finding is that more changes can and will force adaptation in ways that are likely unanticipated by our current understandings. Beyond network penetration and expansion, one of the reasons the Internet is difficult to predict is the applications using the network are being invented almost daily. A few years ago many people had never heard of Twitter. Yet now, Twitter is used to send short messages about everything, from what a person had for breakfast, to coverage of a speech in Congress, or even a government protest. The ability to disseminate moments of political greatness and moments of political disaster through YouTube arrived far more quickly than almost anyone predicted. A misstep caught on video can now be on millions of computer screens shortly after it happens.

Reaching beyond our own findings, bypassing the mass media may be an increasingly important feature of the Internet in future years. The trends today suggest that leading stories may be broken by individuals on the Internet rather than reporters. Iranian students and activists increasingly were the primary source of information through the Internet following their protest of the Iranian presidential elections in 2009 (Newton-Small 2009). CNN now regularly airs and hosts videos created by "citizen" reporters who witness news as it happens. CNN has smartly tried to join its television model with the Internet to remain relevant in the modern era. Traditional reporting may no longer be dominant, with the Internet transmitting events instantaneously with no real controls on content outside draconian efforts by coercive states. Further, the Internet has itself become a media watchdog, as it was Internet bloggers who first challenged CBS about the veracity of the documents it used to challenge then-president George W. Bush's military service in the National Guard (Kurtz 2004). While television is still the dominant form of communication technology in politics and news, the increasing relevance of the Internet may challenge the traditional model and ultimately change how politics is understood and how campaigns are run and covered.

The findings in this book illustrate that the Internet will provoke important changes in American politics. Our data suggest that it will change how we gather information, understand that information, participate, and campaign. As technology expands, it is likely to affect how we vote and even who votes. The uneven expansion of technology will mean the benefits of the Internet will not be universal and some demographic groups will lag. We must be cautious in our assumptions beyond what we have been able to measure and observe, yet the implications of our modern trends are interesting, if difficult to anticipate in the abstract. The Internet allows people to communicate over vast distances with increasingly rapid connections. Programs and ideas that make use of this technology are limited only by human imagination.

It does not even take a programmer to be innovative in its usage. Political opportunists have created some unusual arrangements, including the one proposed by Al Gore and Ralph Nader supporters during the 1994 presidential election. Using forums and websites such as votepair.com (Nussbaum 2004), Nader and Gore voters tried to have Nader voters in competitive states vote for Gore, in return for a Nader vote in non-competitive states. The end result would keep Nader's strength and possibly allow Nader and the Green Party to qualify for matching federal funds in the next election, while helping Gore win the election (Nussbaum 2004). This "Nader Trader" strategy did not prove effective in the election, though it was repeated (with a similar lack of success) in the following electoral contest between John Kerry and George W. Bush in 2000. Nonetheless, it did suggest that the Internet may have different and significant implications because of its power to join individuals across large distances into complex and unpredicted voter behavior.

The power of modern technology such as the Internet is in the way the technology can be used to seize an advantage that would change the balance of power in the political system, thereby changing the results and the policy generated. This might be done through e-voting, or it may be the product of an application of technology that one person or faction properly anticipates and uses, such as the fundraising techniques being adopted currently. Or it simply may be the inability of persons to safeguard the Internet that results in corrupted elections, or a return to earlier campaigning and election techniques that may favor parties or factions with more resources. However politics adapt and change to this new technology, it is clear that the age of the Internet has come, and nothing will be quite the same.

Appendix

CONTROL VARIABLES

Civic Attentiveness (Pew 2006 Post-Election Data and Student Data): "Some people seem to follow what's going on in government and public affairs most of the time, whether there's an election or not. Others aren't that interested. Would you say you follow what's going on in government and public affairs most of the time, some of the time, only now and then, or hardly at all?"

Civic Attentiveness (Pew 2008 Post-Election Data): "How often do you discuss politics and public affairs with others in person, by phone, or by a letter—every day, at least once a week, at least once a month, less than once a month, or never?"

Party Identification (Pew 2006 and 2008 Post-Election and Civic Engagement Data): "In politics today, do you consider yourself a Republican, Democrat, or Independent?" Dummy variables were created for use in multivariate models. (Used in chapters 3, 5, and 6.)

Party Identification (Student Data): "Generally speaking, do you usually think of yourself as a Republican, a Democrat, an Independent, or what?" Dummy variables were created for each available response. Next, partisans were asked: "Would you call yourself a strong (Republican/Democrat) or a not very strong (Republican/Democrat)?" Independents were asked: "Do you think of yourself as closer to the Republican Party or to the Democratic Party, or neither?" This allowed the construction of a seven-point indicator. (Used in chapters 3, 5, and 6.)

Race (Pew 2006 Post-Election Data and Student Data): Race was self-reported. From the Pew Data, we were able to create dummy variables for white, black, Latino, and other race, and from the Student Data, we also included Asian. (Used in chapters 3 and 6.)

Race (Pew 2008 Post-Election and Civic Engagement Data): Race was self-reported. Respondents were asked separately if they were Hispanic. This way they could claim more than one category. We collapsed the variables coding all yes responses to the Hispanic question as Latino. We created dummy variables for white, black, Latino, Asian, and other race. (Used in chapters 3, 5, and 6.)

Gender (Pew 2006 and 2008 Post-Election and Civic Engagement Data and Student Data): Gender was self-reported and coded as 0 male and 1 female. (Used in chapters 3, 5, and 6.)

Income (Pew 2006 and 2008 Post-Election and Civic Engagement Data): Income was self-reported with the following question: "Last year, that is in 2005 (2007), what was your total family income from all sources, before taxes. Just stop me when I get to the right category: less than $10,000; $10,000 to under $20,000; $20,000 to under $30,000; $30,000 to under $40,000; $40,000 to under $50,000; $50,000 to under $75,000; $75,000 to under $100,000; $100,000 or more." This creates an eight-point ordinal scale. For the 2008 data, the response option went up to $150,000 or more, creating a nine-point ordinal scale. (Used in chapters 3, 5, and 6.)

Parents' Finances (Student Data): "Would you say you grew up in a home that was well off financially, somewhere in the middle, or poor?" (Used in chapters 3 and 5.)

Education (Pew 2006 and 2008 Post-Election Data): Respondents were asked to report the last grade or class they completed in school: none; grades 1–8; high school incomplete; high school graduate; technical, trade, or vocational school AFTER high school; some college, no four-year degree; college graduate; postgraduate training/professional school after college. This creates a seven-point ordinal scale. Pew recoded the variable in the Civic Engagement data to be on a four-point scale. (Used in chapters 3, 5, and 6.)

Age (Pew 2006 and 2008 Post-Election and Civic Engagement Data and Student Data): Age was self-reported in both datasets and collapsed into a six-point ordinal scale based on the following age groups: 18–29, 30–39, 40–49, 50–59, and 60 and up. (Used in chapters 3, 5, and 6.)

Student's Major (Student Data): Major was self-reported. A dummy variable was created for students who listed political science. (Used in chapter 3.)

Primary Reason People Rely on the Internet for News (Student Data): "Which of the following comes closest to describing the primary reason why you go online to get news and information? Because getting information online is more convenient; Because you can get information from a wider range of viewpoints; Because you can get more in-depth information on the Web; Because it is more entertaining; Don't go online to get news and information, or Other." (Used in chapter 3.)

Political Participation (Pew 2006 and 2008 Post-Election Data): "A lot of people have been telling us they didn't get a chance to vote in the congressional (congressional was removed in the 2008 data) elections this year on November 7 (4). How about you, did things come up that kept you from voting, or did you happen to vote? (Yes, voted, and No, did not vote)." (Used in chapter 6.)

Political Participation (Pew 2008 Civic Engagement data): The following fifteen items were used to construct an index:
"Please tell me if you have done this in the past twelve months or not. In the past twelve months, have you

- Attended a political rally or speech?
- Attended an organized protest of any kind?
- Attended a political meeting on local, town, or school affairs?
- Worked or volunteered for a political party or candidate?
- Made a speech about a community or political issue?
- Been an active member of any group that tries to influence public policy or government, not including a political party?

- Participated in a walk, run, or ride for a cause?
- Worked with fellow citizens to solve a problem in your community?
- Contacted a national, state, or local government official in person, by phone, or by letter about an issue that is important to you?
- Sent an e-mail to a national, state, or local government official about an issue that is important to you?
- Signed a paper petition?
- Signed a petition online?
- Sent a "letter to the editor" through the U.S. Postal Service to a newspaper or magazine?
- E-mailed a "letter to the editor" or your comments to a newspaper or magazine?
- Called into a live radio or TV show to express an opinion?"

These items scale well together ($\alpha = 0.76$). The ordinal additive index ranges from 0 to 14. (Used in chapter 5.)

Political Participation (Student Data): The following five items were used to construct an index:

- "If the election for president were held today, who would you vote for?" (They were given a list of candidates and a "don't plan to vote" option. We coded them as a zero if they selected "don't plan to vote" and a one if they selected any candidate.)
- "People express their opinions about politics and current events in a number of ways. I'm going to read a list of some of these ways. Thinking only about the last twelve months, have you done any of the following? (no/yes, 0–1)
  A) Contributed money to a candidate running for public office?
  B) Contacted any elected officials?
  C) Joined an organization in support of a particular political issue?
  D) Attended a campaign event?"

These items scale fairly well together ($\alpha = 0.55$). The ordinal additive index ranges from 0 to 5. (Used in chapter 5.)

Vote Choice (Pew 2008 Civic Engagement Data): "In the presidential election, did you vote for the Democratic ticket of Barack Obama and Joe Biden or the Republican ticket of John McCain and Sarah Palin?" Options were rotated. (Used in chapter 5.)

Vote Choice (Student Data): "If the election for president were held today, who would you vote for? (Hillary Clinton, Mike Huckabee, John McCain, Barack Obama)." We coded the Republican candidates (Mike Huckabee and John McCain) as a 0 and the Democratic candidates (Hillary Clinton and Barack Obama) as a 1. Other choices were treated as missing values. (Used in chapter 5.)

Campaign Contact (Pew 2006 Post-Election Data): An index was constructed from the following four items:
"In the past two months, have you (no/yes, 0–1)

- Received mail urging you to vote for a particular candidate?
- Been visited at home by someone urging you to vote for a particular candidate?
- Received prerecorded telephone calls urging you to vote for a particular candidate?
- Received a phone call from a live person urging you to vote for a particular candidate?" (Used in chapter 6.)

Campaign Contact (Pew 2008 Post-Election Data): An index was constructed from the following two items:
"Over the past several months, how often did you

- Receive mail from a candidate or political party? (more than once a day, daily, every few days, once a week, once a month, never)
- Receive e-mail from a candidate or political party? (more than once a day, daily, every few days, once a week, once a month, never)"

Campaign Contact (Pew 2008 Civic Engagement Data): An index was constructed from the following two items:
"How often have you

- Received an e-mail asking you to get involved in a political activity? (daily, every few days, once a week, once a month, never)
- Received a letter asking you to get involved in a political activity? (daily, every few days, once a week, once a month, never)" (Used in chapter 5.)

Notes

CHAPTER 1

1. The development of the Internet was accomplished through government funding, beginning with the Defense Department and continuing through the National Science Foundation (NSF). For a comprehensive review of the history of the Internet consult *The Politics of Internet Communication* by Robert J. Klotz (2004).

CHAPTER 2

1. The operationalization of all additional control variables and dependent variable construction is described in the appendix.

2. While there was not a pervasive problem with missing values in these data, we imputed those few that were to maximize sample size and increase the accuracy of our estimates, especially in the indices and multivariate models. We replaced any missing values in both datasets using the Expectation Maximization (EM) algorithm (Dempster, Laird, and Rubin 1977). This technique finds maximum likelihood estimates in parametric models for incomplete data. The EM algorithm is an iterative procedure that finds the MLE of the parameter vector by first calculating the conditional expectation of the complete-data log likelihood given the observed data and the parameter estimates. Next, it finds the parameter estimates to maximize the complete-data log likelihood from the first step. The two steps are iterated until the iterations converge (for a complete description see Little and Rubin 1987; McLachlan and Krishnan 1997; Schafer 1997).

3. The Senate race for Connecticut included three candidates because Joseph Lieberman, the incumbent, faced challenges from both a Democrat and a Republican candidate. We coded Lieberman as a Democrat for the analysis because he primarily votes with the Democrats. We also coded Bernie Sanders (Democratic Socialist) as a Democrat for the same reason. The Indiana Senate race included a Republican incumbent and a Libertarian challenger. We coded the challenger, Steve Osborn, as a Republican because Libertarians are ideologically closer to Republicans. These three coding choices prevented us from losing cases in the analysis.

4. There were very few missing values. Most of the variables used here had none. We were unable to obtain a Google PageRank for three cases and years holding political office for thirteen. These values were also replaced using the Expectation Maximization (EM) algorithm. While we are aware that data from Wikipedia can be inaccurate, we are not concerned with this problem here because the measures we use from Wikipedia are not controversial. It is used to gather data on the number of years of political experience and the number of years in Congress for each candidate. To validate our measures we took a random sample of 5 percent of the cases of those who won and verified that the data were correct by checking their personal websites available through the U.S. Congress homepage.

5. Actual 2006 and 2008 Pew Indicators used:
   - "Do you use the Internet, at least occasionally? (Yes, No)
   - About how often do you use the Internet (or e-mail, 2008) from home? (several times a day, about once a day, three to five days a week, one to two days a week, every few weeks, less often, never-volunteered)
   - About how often do you use the Internet (or e-mail, 2008) from work? (several times a day, about once a day, three to five days a week, one to two days a week, every few weeks, less often, never-volunteered)."

6. The student survey included this question: "How often do you go online? (more than once a day, every day, three to five days per week, one to two days per week, less often, never)."

7. For some of the analyses later in the book these variables are collapsed where respondents who selected the Internet are coded as a 1 and those who selected all other sources are coded as a 0. This variable is called *Internet primary news source*. "Other" was also given as a response option in the Student Data.

8. The Pew Data had the following items. There are a series of dichotomous (yes/no) items in 2006 and a mix of dichotomous and ordinal indicators in 2008. Indices were constructed for both years:

- 2006 "Did you send or receive e-mails about the candidates or the campaigns—either with personal acquaintances or a political organization—or did you not happen to do this?" 2008 "Over the past several months, how often did you—Send or receive E-MAIL to or from friends, family members, or others about the campaign? (more than once a day, every day, three to five days a week, one to two days a week, less often)"
- 2006 "When you use the Internet, do you ever come across campaign news and information when you may have been going online for a purpose other than to get the news?"
- 2006 "In the months leading up to the November elections, did you hear or read anything online about the following? Did you hear or read anything online about . . . or not?"
- 2008 "Did you get any information online about . . . or not?
  A) Races for U.S. Senate
  B) Races for U.S. House
  C) Races for governor
  D) Local races in your area
  E) Ballot measures or initiatives
  F) The race for president" (2008 only)
- 2006 "There are many different campaign-related activities a person might do on the Internet. I'm going to read a list of things you may or may not have done online in the months leading up to the November elections. Just tell me if you happened to do each one, or not. Did you . . . ?"
- 2008 "I'm going to read a list of things you may or may not have done online in the past year. Did you . . . ?"
  A) 2006 and 2008 "Look for more information online about candidates' positions on the issues or voting records"
  B) 2006 "Look online for candidate endorsements or ratings"
  C) 2006 "Use the Internet to check the accuracy of claims made by or about the candidates"
  D) 2006 "Watch video clips about the candidates or the election that are available online"
     2008 "Watch video online from a campaign or news organization"
  E) 2006 "Sign up to receive e-mail from candidates or campaigns"
     2008 "Sign up online to receive updates about the campaign or the elections"
- 2006 and 2008 "Did you happen to get any news or information about the November elections from the following online sources? Just tell me yes or no after I read each one.

A) Portal news services like Google News or Yahoo News

B) Network TV news websites such as CNN.com, ABCnews.com, or MSNBC.com

C) Websites of major national newspapers such as USAToday.com, the NewYorkTimes.com, or the Wall Street Journal online

D) Websites of local news organizations in your area"

The Student Data also had several items. They are as follows:

- "How often do you go online to get news about the elections? (more than once a day, every day, three to five days per week, one to two days per week, less often, or never)
- Have you sent or received e-mails about the candidates or campaigns?
- When you go online to get information about the ELECTIONS, do you ever do any of the following things?

  A) Participate in online discussions, blogs or 'chat' groups about the elections

  B) Find out about campaign organizations or activities in your area

  C) Read people's political opinions on social networking sites such as MySpace.com or Facebook.com

  D) View political videos on sites such as YouTube.com."

The first of these indicators was standardized between 0 and 1 to give it equal weight with the other yes/no indicators that were coded as 1 for yes and 0 for no.

9. These ordinal indicators were summed to create an ordinal index for later use that ranged from 4 to 16 ($\alpha = 0.71$). We call this index *claim to learn about politics from the Internet.*

10. Less than 1 percent of the respondents answered "yes" instead of filling in the name on the blank provided. We treated this response as "don't know."

11. We coded responses as correct if either first or last name was given regardless of spelling errors.

12. These items were summed creating an ordinal index for the model in chapter 3. It ranged from 0 to -2. While reliability analysis is not needed here because we don't necessarily expect them to scale together (respondents are not expected to be able to answer one question correctly because they can answer another), we performed it anyway. The results suggest that there was a moderate correlation between these three items ($\alpha = 0.50$).

13. The 2008 Pew Civic Engagement data had observations for responses to the following three items (all items were centered between 0 and 1 and an index was constructed $\alpha = 0.50$):

- "Do you ever use a social networking site like MySpace, Facebook, or LinkedIn.com? (If respondent answered yes) Did you happen to do this yesterday, or not?
- Do you ever create or work on your own online journal or blog? (If respondent answered yes) Did you happen to do this yesterday, or not?
- Do you ever use Twitter or another 'micro-blogging' service to share updates about yourself or to see updates about others? (If respondent answered yes) Did you happen to do this yesterday, or not?

The Student Data had observations for the following two items. Both were inverted and recoded to scale between 0 and 1 before constructing an index ($\alpha = 0.58$):

- "How often do you use social networking websites such as MySpace.com or Facebook.com? (more than once a day, every day, three to five days per week, one to two days per week, less often, never)
- How important are social networking websites, such as MySpace.com or Facebook.com, to you for learning about campaigns and candidates? (very important, somewhat important, rarely important, not important)"

14. Both the 2006 and 2008 questions were recoded into dummy variables (1 = "don't have a particular point of view, 0 = all other responses) and called *prefers non-biased news* for use in chapter 6.

15. The available measures of usage were as follows: 1) In the 2006 Pew Data, "Did you happen to get any news or information about the November elections from the following online sources? Just tell me yes or no as I read each one." In the 2008 Pew Data the wording changed slightly, to "Did you happen to get any news or information about the November elections from . . . ? (websites set up by the candidates themselves, issue-oriented websites, online journals or blogs, the website of an alternative news organization such as AlterNet.org or NewsMax.com)." These items were part of a list of thirteen items of which four could be considered one-sided. As necessary, respondents were asked: "Did you get any news or information about the November elections from this source, or not?" Only respondents who answered affirmatively to the question, "Did you get ANY news or information about the November elections on the Internet or through e-mail?" were asked these questions. The alternative news organization sites included in the question were deemed as ideological. AlterNet is from the left. Their aim is to inspire action and advocacy on the environment, human rights and civil liberties, social justice, media, health care issues, and more. NewsMax is from the right. They claim they are considered to be the leading place for conservative web surfers to get their news. We constructed an ordinal index out of these items for use in chapter 6 ($\alpha = 0.46$ for the 2006 data and $\alpha = 0.68$ for the 2008 data). The reliability is not high for the

2006 data but it does not need to be for our purposes as we are not claiming that people who do visit one type site are necessarily likely to visit another, but rather, it is used to gauge the frequency by which respondents visit such sites. Nonetheless, the reliability is high for the 2008 data suggesting that people who do one of these are likely to do the others.

16. See http://en.wikipedia.org/wiki/PageRank for a more thorough description of Google's PageRank.

17. We recoded this variable to range from 0 to 1 for the multivariate analysis in chapter 8.

CHAPTER 3

1. Some contend that neither newspapers nor TV news facilitates learning to any significant degree (Price and Zaller 1993; also see Lichter and Noyes 1995) or, alternatively (and perhaps most plausibly), that it depends less on the medium per se than on the content of the message being delivered (Norris and Sanders 2003; for a slightly different take on this latter point, see Flowers, Haynes, and Crespin 2003).

2. Also, Brundidge and Rice (2009) look at the effect of political knowledge on the heterogeneity of discussion networks at the individual level but do not estimate the effect of information gathering on learning or knowledge.

3. Brundidge and Rice (2009) do suggest that the Internet contributes to the information-rich getting richer but do not directly test whether or not knowledge is actually increased through Internet use.

4. The one exception is the divide across age. Studies typically show that younger people are more active than older (Ranie and Bell 2004). Older people are certainly more likely to fall in the haves category as opposed to the have-nots.

5. The learning indicators were not present in the Pew Data.

6. There were also no knowledge indicators in the Pew Data.

7. The remainder of the statistical analyses using 2006 and 2008 Pew Data in this chapter are based on those surveyed who responded affirmatively to the question about whether or not they had used the Internet for information on the November elections (see chapter 2).

8. We also fit the data to an ordered logit regression model of the learning index with all of these independent variables and there were no significant findings, so the few but apparent bivariate effects washed out when controlling for each.

CHAPTER 4

1. Using flat priors can create pathologies in the resulting posterior distribution. For a detailed explanation see Hobert and Casella (1996).

2. For a more detailed description of the Markov chain convergence tests refer to Cowles and Carlin (1996), Johnson (1996), Robert (1995), and Gelman and Rubin (1992).

CHAPTER 5

1. The question of whether Internet use is related to political participation has been explored using empirical data but primarily not within the U.S. context. Both De Vreese (2007) and Vromen (2007) found that online activities are positively related to political participation in Holland and Australia, respectively. Rice and Katz (2004) do find a relationship between longtime Internet usage and offline forms of political activity in the United States, but they do not look specifically at the effect of social networking on political participation. None of these studies are framed within social networking theory.

2. Political participation is measured as voting in the Pew Data and it is measured as voting and other forms of participation in the Student Data (see appendix).

3. Only the Pew Data had a measure of whether or not the respondent was contacted by a campaign (see appendix).

4. See Dalton (2002), Verba and Nie (1972), and Verba, Schlozman, and Brady (1995) for theoretical justification of the included controls.

5. See *The American Voter* (Campbell et al. 1960) for theoretical justification of the included controls.

6. As noted in chapter 2, we cannot generalize based on the Student Data because they were not randomly selected from the population, but we will speculate here based on the assumption that the data represent younger people.

7. There was no measure of campaign contact in the Student Data.

CHAPTER 6

1. The analyses in this chapter for the 2006 Pew Data are based on data for people who responded affirmatively to the question "Did you get any news or information about the November elections on the Internet or through e-mail?" The questions used to construct the index of usage of biased sites were only given to these

respondents (see chapter 2). For the same reason, the analyses for the 2008 Pew Data are based on people who responded "more than once a day/every day/three to five days per week/one to two days per week/less often" to the question "Did you ever go online to get news or information about the 2008 elections?"

2. See Dalton (2002), Verba and Nie (1972), and Verba, Schlozman, and Brady (1995) for theoretical justification of the included controls.

3. We control here only for those variables that were significant at the 0.05 level in the model of Internet information gathering presented in chapter 3 (table 3.5). There is some change in the significance of these variables, likely a result of the different sample here. The filter question for the analysis is different from that in chapter 3 because the rest of the analysis in this chapter includes measures that are built from data using the filter question stated in note 1. Thus, for consistency within the chapter we used the same filter throughout. We also estimated the model with the chapter 3 filter and the results are substantively consistent with those presented in table 6.1 with the exception that all the controls are significant, so we can be confident that the results are not spurious.

4. These tests are based on the index of the usage of one-sided sites described in chapter 2.

5. Our participation models presented here (table 6.5) do not directly test whether or not consuming one-sided information crystallizes attitudes but the results do conform to the expectation if they did. Zaller (1992) does present theoretical and empirical evidence that consuming one-sided information does crystallize public opinion.

CHAPTER 8

1. People can now obtain government forms and receive instruction over the Internet through websites such as IRS.gov.

2. In open seat races, the candidate who shared the party affiliation of the prior incumbent was treated as the incumbent.

3. One might expect multicollinearity to be an issue because of the relationship between the experience variables and incumbency, but the results suggest that it is not. While the experience variables and incumbency are correlated, they do not cause multicollinearity issues in the multivariate model. In straight OLS models for both Democrats and Republicans, the highest tolerance score was 4.03 (reaching 10 is a problem) and the lowest variation inflation factor 0.25 (.10 or less indicates

a problem) (both for the spending variable in the Republican model). Most were significantly lower and higher respectively.

4. Clearly this estimate seems high considering that the average total votes received in the House races in these data is around 150,000. As mentioned above, the estimates are based on the House and Senate together, so the results are essentially an averaging of the two. As mentioned above, we control for chamber to address the potential that the results are spurious. In a further effort to assure that the results are not chamber dependent, we attempt to estimate separate models for each chamber and party. The problem here is that the sample size becomes too small and several of the variables become constants in the equation. Thus, the models are underspecified. To address this problem, we estimate full models for each party and include the interaction between chamber and web presence. The interaction is insignificant in the Democrat model but is significant at the 0.10 level in the Republican model. Nonetheless, the main effects of web presence are still insignificant in the model. Considered altogether, we do not think that the results are chamber driven.

References

Abramowitz, Alan I. 1975. "Name Familiarity, Reputation, and the Incumbency Effect in a Congressional Election." *Western Political Quarterly* 28 (4): 668–84.

Abramowitz, Alan I. 1991. "Incumbency, Campaign Spending, and the Decline of Competition in U.S. House Elections." *Journal of Politics* 53 (1): 34–56.

Abramson, Paul R. 1983. *Political Attitudes in America.* San Francisco: Freeman.

Achen, Christopher. 1975. "Mass Political Attitudes and the Survey Response." *American Political Science Review* 69 (4): 1218–31.

Aldrich, John H. 1995. *Why Parties?* Chicago: University of Chicago Press.

Alexander, Herbert. 1984. *Financing Politics: Money, Elections, and Political Reform.* Washington, DC: Congressional Quarterly Press.

Allison, Juliann Emmons. 2002. *Technology, Development, and Democracy: International Conflict and Cooperation in the Information Age.* Albany: State University of New York Press.

Althaus, Scott. 1998. "Information Effects in Collective Preferences." *American Political Science Review* 92 (3): 545–58.

Alvarez, R. Michael. 1997. *Information and Elections.* Ann Arbor: University of Michigan Press.

Alvarez, R. Michael, and John Brehm. 1995. "American Ambivalence Towards Abortion Policy: Development of a Heteroskedastic Probit Model of Competing Values." *American Journal of Political Science* 39 (4): 1055–82.

Alvarez, R. Michael, Thad Hall, and Alexander H. Trechsel. 2009. "Internet Voting in Comparative Perspective: The Case of Estonia." *PS: Political Science & Politics* 42 (3): 497–505.

Alvarez, R. Michael, and Jonathan Nagler. 2001. "The Likely Consequences of Internet Voting for Political Representation." *Loyola of Los Angeles Law Review* 34 (3): 1115–52.

Ansolabehere, Stephen, and Shanto Iyengar. 1996. "The Craft of Political Advertising: A Progress Report." In *Political Persuasion and Attitude Change*, eds. D. C. Mutz, P. M. Sniderman, and R. A. Brody. Ann Arbor: University of Michigan Press.

Ansolabehere, Stephen, Shanto Iyengar, Adam Simon, and Nicholas Valentino. 1994. "Does Attack Advertising Demobilize the Electorate?" *American Political Science Review* 88 (4): 829–38.

Anstead, Nick. 2008. "The Internet and Campaign Finance in the U.S. and the U.K.: An Institutional Comparison." *Journal of Information Technology and Politics* 5 (3): 288–302.

Arneil, Barbara. 2006. *Diverse Communities: The Problem with Social Capital.* New York: Cambridge University Press.

Baker, Ross K. 2002. "Examining Senate Individualism versus Senate Folkways in the Aftermath of the Clinton Impeachment." In *U.S. Senate Exceptionalism*, ed. B. Oppenheimer. Columbus: Ohio State University.

Barber, Benjamin R. 2001. "The Uncertainty of Digital Politics." *Harvard International Review* 23 (1): 42–47.

Bardes, Barbara A., and Robert W. Oldendick. 2007. *Public Opinion: Measuring the American Mind.* Belmont, CA: Thomson Wadsworth.

Barnes, James A. 2008. "Online Fundraising Revolution." *National Journal Magazine Online*, April 19.

Barr, Rita. 2004. "Voting on the Internet: Promise and Problems." www.capitol .state.tx.us/hrofr/interim/int76-3.pdf.

Barry, Brian. 1970. *Sociologists, Economists and Democracy*. London: Collier-Macmillan.

Barry, Brian. 1978. *Sociologists, Economists and Democracy*. Chicago: University of Chicago Press.

Bartels, Larry M. 1993. "Messages Received: The Political Impact of Media Exposure." *American Political Science Review* 87 (2): 267–85.

Beatson, J. W. 1912. *The National Economic League, the Initiative and Referendum: Arguments Pro and Con*. Cambridge, MA: Caustic-Claflin Co., Printers.

Bennett, W. Lance. 2004. *News: The Politics of Illusion*. 6th ed. New York: Longman.

Bennett, W. Lance. 2008. *News: The Politics of Illusion*. 8th ed. New York: Longman.

Best, Samuel J., and Brian S. Krueger. "Online Interactions and Social Capital: Distinguishing Between New and Existing Ties." *Social Science Computer Review* 24:395–410.

Bimber, Bruce. 1998. "The Internet and Political Transformation: Populism, Community, and Accelerated Pluralism." *Polity* 31 (1): 133–60.

Bimber, Bruce. 2001. "Information and Political Engagement in America: The Search for Effects of Information Technology at the Individual Level." *Political Research Quarterly* 54 (1): 53–67.

Bimber, Bruce A., and Richard Davis. 2003 *Campaigning Online: The Internet in U.S. Elections*. Oxford; New York: Oxford University Press.

Berelson, Bernard R., Paul F. Lazarsfeld, and William N. McPhee. 1954. *Voting: A Study of Opinion Formation in a Presidential Campaign*. Chicago: University of Chicago Press.

Berkowitz, Dan, and David Pritchard. 1989. "Political Knowledge and Communication Resources." *Journalism Quarterly* 66 (3): 697–701.

Blais, André. 2000. *To Vote or Not to Vote? The Merits and Limits of Rational Choice Theory*. Pittsburgh: University of Pittsburgh Press.

Bolton, Alexander. 2005. "Fundraisers Jilt Dean." *The Hill*, June 7.

Bond, Jon R., Cary Covington, and Richard Fleisher. 1985. "Explaining Challenger Quality in Congressional Elections." *Journal of Politics* 47 (2): 510–29.

Bonin, A. (2007). "Small dollars and max donors, part II". *Daily Kos*, July 16. Retrieved April 1, 2010, from http://www.dailykos.com/storyonly/2007/7/16/155836/361.

Breaux, David A., and Anthony Gierzynski. 1991. "'It's Money That Matters': Campaign Expenditures and State Legislative Primaries." *Legislative Studies Quarterly* 16 (3): 429–43.

Brennan, Linda L., and Victoria Johnson. 2004. *Social, Ethical and Policy Implications of Information Technology*. Hershey, PA: Information Science Publishing.

Browder, Rebekah (2006). "Internet Voting with Initiatives and Referendums: Stumbling towards Direct Democracy." *Seattle University Law Review* 29 (2): 485–514.

Browning, Graeme. 2002. *Electronic Democracy: Using the Internet to Transform American Politics*. 2nd ed. Medford, NJ: CyberAge Books.

Buchanan, Bruce. 1991. *Electing a President: The Markle Commission Research on Campaign '88*. Austin: University of Texas Press.

Burnham, Walter Dean. 1987. "The Turnout Problem." In *Elections American Style*, ed. A. J. Reichley. Washington, DC: Brookings Institution.

Campbell, Angus, Philip E. Converse, Warren E. Miller, and Donald E. Stokes. 1960. *The American Voter*. New York: John Wiley and Sons.

Chadwick, Andrew. 2006. *Internet Politics: States, Citizens, and New Communication Technologies*. New York: Oxford University Press.

Chaffee, Steven H., and Joan Schleuder. 1986. "Measurement and Effects of Attention to Media News." *Human Communication Research* 13 (1): 76–107.

Chaffee, Steven H., Xinshu Zhao, and Glenn Leshner. 1994. "Political Knowledge and the Campaign Media of 1992." *Communication Research* 21 (3): 305–24.

Choi, Hyeon C., and Samuel L. Becker. 1987. "Media Use, Issue/Image Discriminations, and Voting." *Communication Research* 14 (3): 267–91.

Coleman, Stephen, and John Gotze. 2001. *Bowling Together: Online Public Engagement in Policy Deliberation*. London: Hansard Society.

Coleman, Stephen, and N. Hall. 2001. "Spinning on the Web: E-Campaigning and Beyond." In *2001 Cyber Space Odyssey: The Internet in the UK Election*, ed. S. Coleman. London: Hansard Society.

Converse, Philip E. 1964. "The Nature of Belief Systems in Mass Publics." In *Ideology and Discontent*, ed. D. E. Apter. New York: Free Press.

Conway, Margaret. 1991. *Political Participation in the United States*. Washington, DC: Congressional Quarterly Press.

Cornfeld, Michael, Lee Rainie, and John Horrigan. 2003. "Untuned Keyboards: Online Campaigners, Citizens and Portals in the 2002 Elections." In *Pew Internet and American Life Project*.

Corrado, Anthony, and Charles M. Firestone. 1996. "Elections in Cyberspace: Promises and Perils." In *Elections in Cyberspace: Toward a New Era in American Politics*, eds. A. Corrado and C. M. Firestone. Washington, DC: The Aspen Institute.

Cowles, Mary K., and Bradley P. Carlin. 1996. "Markov Chain Monte Carlo Convergence Diagnostics: A Comparative Review." *Journal of the American Statistical Association* 91 (434): 883–904.

Cox, Gary W., and Mathew D. McCubbins. 1993. *Legislative Leviathan: Party Government in the House*. Berkeley and Los Angeles: University of California Press.

Cox, Gary W., and Scott Morgenstern. 1995. "The Incumbency Advantage in Multimember Districts: Evidence from the U.S. States." *Legislative Studies Quarterly* 20 (3): 329–49.

Craig, Stephen C., and Michael D. Martinez, eds. 2005a. *Ambivalence, Politics, and Public Policy*. New York: Palgrave Macmillan.

Craig, Stephen C., and Michael D. Martinez, eds. 2005b. *Ambivalence and the Structure of Political Opinion*. New York: Palgrave Macmillan.

Dalton, Russell J. 2002. *Citizen Politics: Public Opinion and Political Participation in Advanced Industrial Democracies*, 3rd ed. New York: Chatham House.

Dalton, Russell J. 2006. *Citizen Politics: Public Opinion and Political Participation in Advanced Industrial Democracies*, 4th ed. New York: Chatham House.

Davis, Richard. 1999. *The Web of Politics: The Internet's Impact on the American Political System*. New York: Oxford University Press.

De Vreese, Claes H. 2007. "Digital Renaissance: Young Consumer and Citizen?" *The Annals of the American Academy of Political and Social Science* 611 (1): 207–16.

Delli Carpini, Michael X., and Scott Keeter. 1996. *What Americans Know about Politics and Why It Matters*. New Haven, CT: Yale University Press.

Dempster, Arthur P., Nan M. Laird, and Donald B. Rubin. 1977. "Maximum Likelihood from Incomplete Data via the EM Algorithm." *Journal of the Royal Statistical Society* 39 (1): 1–38.

Dodd, Lawrence C. 1981. *Congress, the Constitution and the Crisis of Legitimation*. In *Congress Reconsidered*, eds. L. C. Dodd and B. I. Oppenheimer. Washington, DC: CQ Press.

Downs, Anthony. 1957. *An Economic Theory of Democracy*. New York: Harper.

Dulio, David A., Donald L. Goff, and James A. Thurber. 1999. "Untangled Web: Internet Use during the 1998 Election." *PS: Political Science and Politics* 32 (1): 53–59.

Eagly, Alice H., and Shelly Chaiken. 1993. *The Psychology of Attitudes*. Fort Worth, TX: Harcourt Brace.

Erikson, Robert S., and Thomas R. Palfrey. 1998. "Campaign Spending and Incumbency: An Alternative Simultaneous Equations Approach." *Journal of Politics* 60 (2): 355–73.

Evans, C. Lawrence. 2002. "How Senators Decide: An Exploration." In *Senate Exceptionalism*, ed. B. Oppenheimer. Columbus: Ohio State University Press.

Festinger, Leon. 1957. *A Theory of Cognitive Dissonance*. Stanford, CA: Stanford University Press.

Fiorina, Morris P. 1989. *Congress: Keystone of the Washington Establishment*. New Haven, CT: Yale University Press.

Fiorina, Morris, Samuel J. Abrams, and Jeremy C. Pope. 2006. *Culture War? The Myth of a Polarized America*. New York: Pearson Education.

Flowers, Julianne F., Audrey A. Haynes, and Michael H. Crespin. 2003. "The Media, the Campaign, and the Message." *American Journal of Political Science* 47 (2): 259–73.

Foot, Kirsten A., and Steven M. Schneider. 2006. *Web Campaigning*. Boston: MIT Press.

Foot, Kirsten, Steven Schneider, Meghan Dougherty, Elena Larsen, and Michael Xenos. 2003. "Analyzing Linking Practices: Candidate Sites in the 2002 U.S.

Electoral Web Sphere." *Journal of Computer-Mediated Communication* 8 (4). Retrieved December 30, 2010, from http://jcmc.indiana.edu/vol8/issue4/foot.html.

Fox, Susannah. 2005. "Digital Divisions." In *Pew Internet and American Life Project.*

Franklin, Charles H. 1991. "Eschewing Obfuscation? Campaigns and the Perception of U.S. Senate Incumbents." *American Political Science Review* 85 (4): 1193–1214.

Franklin, Mark N. 1996. "Electoral Participation." In *Controversies in Voting Behavior*, eds. R. G. Niemi and H. F. Weisberg. Washington, DC: CQ Press.

Freedman, Des. 2006. "Internet Transformations: 'Old' Media Resilience in the 'New Media' Revolution." In *Media and Cultural Theory*, eds. J. Curran and D. Morley. Abingdon: Routledge.

Gainous, Jason, and Kevin Wagner. 2007. "The Electronic Ballot Box: A Rational Voting Model and the Internet." *American Review of Politics* 28 (Spring and Summer): 19–35.

Gallen, Jonathan. 2005. "The End of the Chads? The Future of Internet Voting in America." Paper presented at the annual meeting of the Southwestern Political Science Association, New Orleans, LA, Fairmont Hotel, March 23. Retrieved May 25, 2010, from http://www.allacademic.com/meta/p88872_index.html.

Gelman, Andrew, and Donald B. Rubin. 1992. "Inference from Iterative Simulation Using Multiple Sequences." *Statistical Science* 7 (4): 457–72.

Gerber, Alan S., and Donald P. Green. 2000. "The Effects of Canvassing, Telephone Calls, and Direct Mail on Voter Turnout: A Field Experiment." *American Political Science Review* 94 (3): 653–63.

Geweke, John. 1993. "Bayesian Treatment of the Independent Student t-Linear Model." *Journal of Applied Econometrics* 8 (S): S19–40.

Gibson, Rachel, and Stephen Ward. 1998. "U.K. Political Parties and the Internet: 'Politics as Usual' in the New Media?" *The Harvard International Journal of Press/Politics* 3 (3): 14–38.

Gibson, William. 1985. *Neuromancer.* London: Victor Gollancz.

Gill, Jeff. 2002. *Bayesian Methods for the Social and Behavioral Sciences.* Boca Raton, FL: Chapman and Hall/CRC.

Gill, Jeff, and Jason Gainous. 2002. "Why Does Voting Get So Complicated? A Review of Theories for Analyzing Democratic Participation." *Statistical Science* 17 (4): 1–22.

Gillman, Howard. 2003. *The Only Votes That Counted: How the Court Decided the 2000 Presidential Election.* Chicago: University of Chicago Press.

Gingrich, Newt. 2009. "Supreme Court Nominee Sotomayor: You Read, You Decide." *Human Events,* June 3.

Gould, Jack. 1946. "Television: Boon or Bane." *Public Opinion Quarterly* 10 (3): 314–20.

Graber, Doris A. 1988. *Processing the News: How People Tame the Information Tide.* White Plains, NY: Longman.

Graber, Doris A. 2001. *Processing Politics: Learning from Television in the Internet Age.* Chicago: University of Chicago Press.

Graber, Doris A. 2006. *Mass Media & American Politics.* Washington, DC: CQ Press.

Graber, Doris A. 2007. *Media Power in Politics.* Washington, DC: CQ Press.

Graf, Joseph, Grant Reeher, Michael Malbin, and Costas Panagopoulos. 2006. "Small Donors and Online Giving: A Study of Donors to the 2004 Presidential Campaigns." Report published by the Institute for Politics, Democracy & the Internet, March 2006.

Green, Donald Philip, and Jonathan S. Krasno. 1988. "Salvation for the Spendthrift Incumbent: Re-estimating the Effects of Campaign Spending in House Elections." *American Journal of Political Science* 32 (4): 884–907.

Green, Donald P., and Ian Shapiro. 1996. *Pathologies of Rational Choice Theory: A Critique of Applications in Political Science.* New Haven, CT: Yale University Press.

Grenzke, Janet. 1989. "PACs and the Congressional Supermarket: The Currency Is Complex." *American Journal of Political Science* 33 (1): 1–24.

Habermas, Jürgen. 1991. *The Structural Transformation of the Public Sphere: An Inquiry into a Category of Bourgeois Society (Studies in Contemporary German Social Thought).* Boston: MIT Press.

Hadari, Saguiv A. 1989. "Unintended Consequences in Periods of Transition: Tocqueville's 'Recollections Revisited.'" *American Journal of Political Science* 33 (1): 136–49.

Hagen, Michael G., and William G. Mayer. 2000. "The Modern Politics of Presidential Selection: How Changing the Rules Really Did Change the Game." In *In Pursuit of the White House 2000: How We Choose Our Presidential Nominees*, ed. W. G. Meyer. New York: Chatham House.

Hegel, Georg Wilhelm Friedrich, and Walter Arnold Kaufmann. 1977. *Hegel: Texts and Commentary: Hegel's Preface to His System in a New Translation with Commentary on Facing Pages, and "Who Thinks Abstractly?"* Notre Dame, IN: University of Notre Dame Press.

Helman, S. 2007. "Internet-based PAC Driving Democratic Push." *Boston Globe*, August 7. Retrieved August 23, 2007, from http://www.boston.com/news/local/massachusetts/articles/2007/08/07/internet_based_pac_driving_democratic_push/.

Hill, Kevin A., and John E. Hughes. 1998. *Cyberpolitics*. New York: Rowman & Littlefield.

Hobert, James P., and George Casella. 1996. "The Effect of Improper Priors on Gibbs Sampling in Hierarchical Linear Mixed Models." *Journal of the American Statistical Association* 91 (436): 1461–73.

Hohenstein, Kurt. 2007. *Coining Corruption: The Making of the American Campaign Finance System*. Dekalb, IL: Northern Illinois University Press.

Holbrook, Thomas M., and Charles M. Tidmarch. 1993. "The Effects of Leadership Positions on Votes for Incumbents in State Legislative Elections." *Political Research Quarterly* 46 (4): 897–909.

Horrigan, John B. 2001. "Online Communities: Networks That Nurture Long-Distance Relationships and Local Ties." In *Pew Internet and American Life Project*.

Horrigan, John B., and Lee Rainie. 2002. "The Broadband Difference: How Online Behavior Changes with High-Speed Internet Connections at Home." In *Pew Internet and American Life Project*.

Isikoff, Michael. 2008. "Obama's 'Good Will' Hunting." *Newsweek*, October 4.

Jackman, Simon. 2000. "Estimation and Inference via Bayesian Simulation: An Introduction to Markov Chain Monte Carlo." *American Journal of Political Science* 44 (2): 375–404.

Jacobson, Gary C. 1990. "The Effects of Campaign Spending in House Elections: New Evidence for Old Arguments." *American Journal of Political Science* 34 (2): 334–62.

Jacobson, Gary C. 1992. *The Politics of Congressional Elections*, 3rd ed. New York: HarperCollins.

Johnson, Thomas, and Barbara Kaye. 2003. "A Boost or Bust for Democracy? How the Web Influenced Political Attitudes and Behaviors in 1996 and 2000 Presidential Elections." *International Journal of Press/Politics* 8 (3): 9–34.

Johnson, Valen E. 1996. "Studying Convergence of Markov Chain Monte Carlo Algorithms Using Coupled Sample Paths." *Journal of the American Statistical Association* 91 (433): 154–66.

Jones, Sydney, and Susannah Fox. 2009. "Pew Internet Project Data Memo." In *Pew Internet and American Life Project.*

Kernell, Samuel. 1997. *Going Public: New Strategies of Presidential Leadership*, 3rd ed. Washington, DC: Congressional Quarterly Press.

Kernell, Samuel. 2006. *Going Public: New Strategies of Presidential Leadership*, 4th ed. Washington, DC: Congressional Quarterly Press.

Khan, Huma, and Jake Tapper. 2009. "Newt Gingrich on Twitter: Sonia Sotomayor 'Racist,' Should Withdraw." ABC News, May 27.

King, Anthony. 1997. *Running Scared.* New York: Free Press.

Klotz, Robert J. 2004. *The Politics of Internet Communication.* Lanham, MD: Rowman & Littlefield.

Kobrak, Peter. 2002. *Cozy Politics: Political Parties, Campaign Finance, and Compromised Elections.* Boulder, CO: Lynne Rienner.

Koetzle, William. 1998. "The Impact of Constituency Diversity upon the Competitiveness of U.S. House Elections, 1962–96." *Legislative Studies Quarterly* 23 (4): 561–73.

Krebs, Timothy B. 1998. "The Determinants of Candidates' Vote Share and the Advantages of Incumbency in City Council Elections." *American Journal of Political Science* 42 (3): 921–35.

Krueger, Brian S. 2002. "Assessing the Potential of Internet Political Participation in the United States." *American Politics Research* 30 (5): 476–98.

Krueger, Brian S. 2006. "A Comparison of Conventional and Internet Political Mobilization." *American Politics Research* 34 (6): 759–76.

Lee, Peter M. 1989. *Bayesian Statistics: An Introduction*. New York: Oxford University Press.

Lee, Frances E., and Bruce I. Oppenheimer. 1999. *Sizing Up the Senate: The Unequal Consequences of Equal Representation*. Chicago: University of Chicago Press.

Leighley, Jan E., and Jonathan Nagler. 1992. "Socioeconomic Bias in Turnout 1964–1988: The Voters Remain the Same." *American Political Science Review* 86 (3): 725–36.

Leighley, Jan E., and Arnold Vedlitz. 1999. "Race, Ethnicity, and Political Participation: Competing Models and Contrasting Explanations." *Journal of Politics* 61 (4): 1092–1114.

Levitt, Steven D., and Catherine D. Wolfram. 1997. "Decomposing the Sources of Incumbency Advantage in the U.S. House." *Legislative Studies Quarterly* 22 (1): 45–60.

Lichter, S. Robert, and Richard E. Noyes. 1995. *Good Intentions Make Bad News: Why Americans Hate Campaign Journalism*. Lanham, MD: Rowman & Littlefield.

Little, Roderick J. A., and Donald B. Rubin. 1987. *Statistical Analysis with Missing Data*. New York: John Wiley & Sons.

Lowenstein, Daniel H. 1989. "On Campaign Finance Reform: The Root of All Evil Is Deeply Rooted." *Hofstra Law Review* 18: 301–67.

Lupia, Arthur, and Zoe Baird. 2003. "Can Websites Change Citizens? Implications of Web, White and Blue in 2000." *Political Science and Politics* 36:77–82.

Lupia, Arthur, and Tasha S. Philpot. 2007. "Views from inside the Net: How Websites Affect Young Adults' Political Interest." *Journal of Politics* 67 (4): 1122–42.

Lusoli, Wainer. 2005. "A Second-Order Medium? The Internet as a Source of Electoral Information in 25 European Countries." *Information Polity* 10 (3/4): 247–65.

Lusoli, Wainer, and Janelle Ward. 2005. "'Politics Makes Strange Bedfellows': The Internet in the 2004 European Parliament Election." *The Harvard International Journal of Press/Politics* 10 (4): 71–97.

Malbin, Michael. 1984. "Looking Back at the Future of Campaign Finance Reform." In *Money and Politics in the United States*, ed. M. Malbin. Chatham, NJ.: Chatham House.

Margolis, Michael, and David Resnick. 2000. *Politics as Usual: The Cyberspace Revolution.* London: Sage.

Marrero, Diana. 2009. "Congress Joins Twitter Craze." *Milwaukee Journal Sentinel,* April 13.

Martinez, Michael D., and David Hill. 1999. "Did Motor Voter Work?" *American Politics Quarterly* 27 (3): 296–315.

McBride, Allan. 1998. "Television, Individualism, and Social Capital." *Political Science and Politics* 31 (3): 543–52.

McDonald, Michael P., and Samuel L. Popkin. 2001. "The Myth of the Vanishing Voter." *American Political Science Review* 95 (4): 963–74.

McLeod, Jack M., Zhongshi Guo, Katie Daily, Catherine A. Steele, Huiping Huang, Edward Horowitz, and Huailin Chen. 1996. "The Impact of Traditional and Nontraditional Media Forms in the 1992 Presidential Election." *Journalism and Mass Communication Quarterly* 73 (2): 401–16.

McLachlan, Geoffrey J., and Thriyambakam Krishnan. 1997. *The EM Algorithm and Extensions.* New York: John Wiley & Sons.

Memmott, Mark, and Jill Lawrence. 2008. "'Yes We Can' Has Topped 3.7M Views." *USA Today,* February 6.

Morris, Dick. 1999. *Vote.com: How Big-Money Lobbyists and the Media Are Losing Their Influence, and the Internet Is Giving Power Back to the People.* Los Angeles: Renaissance Books.

Mossberger, Karen, Caroline J. Tolbert, and Mary Stansbury. 2003. *Virtual Inequality: Beyond the Digital Divide.* Washington, DC: Georgetown University Press.

Mossberger, Karen, Caroline J. Tolbert, and Ramona S. McNeal. 2008. *Digital Citizenship: The Internet, Society, and Participation.* Cambridge: MIT Press.

Moussalli, Stephanie D. 1990. *Campaign Finance Reform: The Case for Deregulation.* Tallahassee, FL.: James Madison Institute.

Moy, Patricia, and Michael Pfau. 2000. *With Malice Toward All? The Media and Public Confidence in Democratic Institutions.* Westport, CT: Praeger.

Mutch, Robert E. 1988. *Campaigns, Congress, and Courts: The Makings of Federal Campaign Finance Law.* New York: Praeger.

Nathan, Sara. 2000. "More Investors Click to Cast Proxy Votes." *USA Today*, March 27.

Neuman, Russell, Marion R. Just, and Ann N. Crigler. 1992. *Common Knowledge: News and the Construction of Political Meaning*. Chicago: University of Chicago Press.

Newton-Small, Jay. 2009. "Political Tweets." Time Magazine Online, June 27.

Nie, Norman H., Jane Junn, and Kenneth Stehlik-Barry. *Education and Democratic Citizenship in America*. Chicago: University of Chicago Press.

Norris, Pippa. 2001. *Digital Divide: Civic Engagement, Information Poverty, and the Internet Worldwide*. Cambridge: Cambridge University Press.

Norris, Pippa. 2002. *Democratic Phoenix: Reinventing Political Activism*. New York: Cambridge University Press.

Norris, Pippa, and David Sanders. 2003. "Message or Medium? Campaign Learning During the 2001 British General Election." *Political Communication* 20 (3): 233–62.

Nussbaum, Paul. 2004. "A Kerry for a Nader? Vote-trading Gears Up." *The Philadelphia Inquirer*, September 20.

O'Reilly, Bill. 2006. *Culture Warrior*. New York: Broadway Books.

Page, Benjamin I., and Robert Y. Shapiro. 1992. "The Rational Public: Fifty Years of Trends in Americans' Policy Preferences." In *Controversies in Voting Behavior*, eds. R. G. Niemi and H. F. Weisberg. Washington, DC: CQ Press.

Patterson, Thomas E. 1980. *The Mass Media Election*. New York: Praeger.

Patterson, Thomas E. 2007. "Creative Destruction: An Exploratory Look at News on the Internet." A report from the Joan Shorenstein Center on the Press, Politics, and Public Policy, John F. Kennedy School of Government. Boston: Harvard University.

Patterson, Thomas E., and Robert D. McClure. 1976. *The Unseeing Eye: The Myth of Television Power in National Elections*. New York: Putnam.

Petrocik, John R., and Scott W. Desposato. 2004. "Incumbency and Short-Term Influences on Voters." *Political Research Quarterly* 57 (3): 363–73.

Pollard, William E. 1986. *Bayesian Statistics for Evaluation Research: An Introduction*. Beverly Hills, CA: Sage.

Popkin, Samuel. 1991. *The Reasoning Voter.* Chicago: University of Chicago Press.

Portes, Alejandro. 1998. "Social Capital: Its Origins and Applications in Modern Sociology." *Annual Review of Sociology* 24:1–24.

Postman, Neil. 1985. *Amusing Ourselves to Death: Public Discourse in the Age of Show Business.* New York: Viking Penguin.

Powell Jr., G. Bingham. 1986. "American Voter Turnout in Comparative Perspective." *American Political Science Review* 80 (1): 17–43.

Prevost, Alicia Kolar, and Brian Schaffner. 2008. "Digital Divide or Just Another Absentee Ballot." *American Politics Research* 36 (4): 510–29.

Price, Vincent, and John Zaller. 1993. "Who Gets the News? Alternative Measures of News Reception and Their Implications for Research." *Public Opinion Quarterly* 57 (2): 133–64.

Putnam, Robert D. 1995a. "Tuning In, Tuning Out: The Strange Disappearance of Social Capital in America." In *Controversies in Voting Behavior,* eds. R. G. Niemi and H. F. Weisberg. Washington, DC: CQ Press.

Putnam, Robert D. 1995b. "Bowling Alone: America's Declining Social Capital." *Journal of Democracy* 6 (1): 65–78.

Putnam, Robert D. 2000. *Bowling Alone: The Collapse and Revival of American Community.* New York: Simon & Schuster.

Rainie, Lee, and Peter Bell. 2004. "The Numbers That Count." *New Media and Society* 6 (1): 44–54.

Rainie, Lee, and John B. Horrigan. 2007. "Election 2006 Online." In *Pew Internet and American Life Project.*

Rash, Wayne. 1997. *Politics on the Nets: Wiring the Political Process.* New York: Freeman.

Rich, Frank. 2008. "Next Up for the Democrats: Civil War." *New York Times,* February 10.

Rice, Ronald E., and James Everett Katz. 2004. "The Internet and Political Involvement in 1996 and 2000." In *Society Online: The Internet in Context,* eds. P. Howard and S. Jones. Thousand Oaks, CA: Sage.

Riker, William H. 1986. *The Art of Political Manipulation.* New Haven, CT: Yale University Press.

Riker, William H., and Peter C. Ordeshook. 1968. "A Theory of the Calculus of Voting." *American Political Science Review* 62 (1): 25–42.

Robert, Christian P. 2001. *The Bayesian Choice: A Decision Theoretic Motivation.* New York: Springer-Verlag.

Robert, Christian P. 1995. "Convergence Control Methods for Markov Chain Monte Carlo Algorithms." *Statistical Science* 10 (3): 231–53.

Robinson, John P., and Mark K. Levy. 1986. *The Main Source: Learning from Television News.* Beverly Hills, CA: Sage.

Rosenstone, Steven J., and John Mark Hansen. 1993. *Mobilization, Participation, and Democracy in America.* New York: Macmillan.

Sabatier, Paul. 1992. "Interest Group Membership and Organization: Multiple Theories." In *The Politics of Interest,* ed. M. Petracca. Boulder, CO: Westview Press.

Sabato, Larry. 1987. "Real and Imagined Corruption in Campaign Financing." In *Elections American Style,* ed. A. J. Reichley. Washington, DC: Brookings Institution.

Saco, Diana. 2002. *Cybering Democracy: Public Space and the Internet, Electronic Mediations.* Minneapolis: University of Minnesota Press.

Salant, Jonathan D. 2000. "Bush Campaign Last in Internet Fund-Raising." Associated Press, February 5.

Samples, John. 2006. *The Fallacy of Campaign Finance Reform.* Chicago: University of Chicago Press.

Sartre, Jean-Paul. 1976. *Critique of Dialectical Reason, Theory of Practical Ensembles.* London; Atlantic Highlands, NJ: NLB; Humanities Press.

Schafer, Joseph L. 1997. *Analysis of Incomplete Multivariate Data.* New York: Chapman and Hall.

Schickler, Eric. 2001. *Disjointed Pluralism: Institutional Innovation and the Development of the U.S. Congress.* Princeton, NJ: Princeton University Press.

Schlozman, Kay Lehman, Sidney Verba, and Henry E. Brady. 2010. "Weapon of the Strong? Participatory Inequality and the Internet." *Perspectives on Politics* 8 (2): 487–509.

Schneider, Steven, and Kirsten Foot. 2002. "Online Structure for Political Action: Exploring Presidential Campaign Websites from the 2000 Presidential Election." *Javnost/The Public* 9 (2): 43–60.

Selnow, Gary W. 1998. *Electronic Whistle-Stops: The Impact of the Internet on American Politics*. Praeger Series in Political Communication. Westport, CT: Praeger.

Shapiro, Andrew L. 1999. *The Control Revolution: How the Internet Is Putting Individuals in Charge and Changing the World We Know*. New York: Public Affairs.

Shepsle, Kenneth. 1989. "The Changing Textbook Congress." In *Can the Government Govern?*, eds. J. E. Chubb and P. E. Peterson. Washington, DC: Brookings Institution.

Sinclair, Barbara. 1989. *The Transformation of the U.S. Senate*. Baltimore: Johns Hopkins University Press.

Sinclair, Barbara. 2001. "The World of U.S. Senators." In *Congress Reconsidered*, ed. L. C. Dodd. Washington, DC: CQ Press.

Singel, Ryan, and Kevin Poulsen. 2006. "Your Own Personal Internet." Wired.com, June 29.

Smith, Adam. 1991. *Wealth of Nations*. Great Minds Series. Buffalo, NY: Prometheus Books.

Smith, Bradley A. 2001. *Unfree Speech: The Folly of Campaign Finance Reform*. Princeton, NJ: Princeton University Press.

Smith, Rodney A. 2006. *Money, Power and Elections: How Campaign Finance Reform Subverts American Democracy*. Baton Rouge: Louisiana State University Press.

Smith, Stephen A. 1994. *Bill Clinton on Stump, State, and Stage: The Rhetorical Road to the White House*. Fayetteville: University of Arkansas Press.

Solop, Frederic I. 2000. "Public Support for Internet Voting: Are We Falling into a 'Racial Ravine?'" Paper presented at the American Association of Public Opinion Research, Portland, Oregon.

Solop, Frederic I. 2001. "Digital Democracy Comes of Age: Internet Voting and the 2000 Arizona Democratic Primary Election." *Political Science and Politics* 34 (2): 289–93.

Sommers, Paul M. 2002. "Is Presidential Greatness Related to Height?" *The College Mathematics Journal* 33 (1): 14–16.

Sorauf, Frank J. 1988. *Money in American Elections.* New Haven, CT: Yale University Press.

Sparks, Colin. 2000. "Media Theory after the Fall of European Communism: Why the Old Models from East and West Won't Do Anymore." In *De-Westernizing Media Systems,* eds. J. Curran and M. J. Parks. London: Routledge.

Squire, Peverill. 1989. "Challengers in U.S. Senate Elections." *Legislative Studies Quarterly* 14 (4): 531–37.

Stanyer, James. 2008. "Web 2.0 and the Transformation of News and Journalism." In *The Handbook of Internet Politics,* eds. A. Chadwick and P. N. Howard. London: Routledge.

Steele, Cherie, and Arthur Stein. 2002. "Communications Revolutions and International Relations." In *Technology, Development and Democracy,* ed. Juliann Emmons Allison. Albany: State University of New York Press.

Stromer-Galley, Jennifer. 2000. "Democratizing Democracy: Strong Democracy, U.S. Political Campaigns and the Internet." In *The Internet, Democracy and Democratization,* ed. P. Ferdinand. London: Frank Cass.

Sunstein, Cass. 2001. *Republic.com.* Princeton, NJ: Princeton University Press.

Teachout, Zephyr, and Thomas Streeter. 2007. *Mousepads, Shoe Leather, and Hope.* Boulder, CO: Paradigm.

Tewksbury, David H. 2003. "What Do Americans Really Want to Know? Tracking the Behavior of News Readers on the Internet." *Journal of Communication* 53 (4): 694–710.

Tewksbury, David H. 2005. "The Seeds of Audience Fragmentation: Specialization in the Use of Online News Sites." *Journal of Broadcasting & Electronic Media* 49 (3): 332–48.

Tewksbury, David H., and Jason Rittenberg. 2008. "News on the Internet: Audience Selection, Consumption, and Retention of Public Affairs News." In *The Handbook of Internet Politics,* eds. A. Chadwick and P. N. Howard. London: Routledge.

Tolbert, Caroline J., and Ramona S. McNeal. 2003. "Unraveling the Effects of the Internet on Political Participation?" *Political Research Quarterly* 56 (2): 175–85.

Tocqueville, Alexis. 2000. *Democracy in America.* Indianapolis: Hackett.

Trippi, Joe. 2004. *The Revolution Will Not Be Televised: Democracy, the Internet and the Overthrow of Everything.* New York: HarperCollins.

Tullock, Gordon. 1967. *Toward Mathematics of Politics.* Ann Arbor: University of Michigan Press.

United States Department of Commerce. 2000. "Falling Through the Net: Toward Digital Inclusion." A Report on Americans' Access to Technology Tools. Washington, DC: Department of Commerce.

United States Department of Commerce. 2002. "A Nation Online: How Americans Are Expanding Their Use of the Internet." Washington, DC: Department of Commerce.

United States Department of Commerce, Bureau of the Census. 2000. "Statistical Abstract of the United States." Washington, DC: Government Printing Office.

Van Alstyne, Marshall, and Erik Brynjolfsson. 2005. "Global Village or Cyberbalkans: Modeling and Measuring the Integration of Electronic Communities." *Management Science* 51 (6): 851–68.

Vargas, Jose Antonio. 2008. "Obama Raised Half a Billion Online." *Washington Post*, November 20.

Verba, Sidney, and Norman H. Nie. 1972. *Participation in America: Political Democracy and Social Equality.* New York: Harper and Row.

Verba, Sidney, Kay Lehman Schlozman, and Henry E. Brady. 1995. *Voice and Equality: Civic Voluntarism in American Politics.* Cambridge: Harvard University Press.

Verba, Sidney, Kay Lehman Schlozman, Henry Brady, and Norman H. Nie. 1993. "Race, Ethnicity and Political Resources: Participation in the United States." *British Journal of Political Science* 23 (4): 453–97.

Vromen, Ariadne. 2007. "Australian Young People's Participatory Practices and Internet Use." *Information, Communication & Society* 10 (1): 48–68.

Wagner, Kevin M., and Eric Prier. "The Legislature and the Legislative Process in Florida." In *Government and Politics in Florida*, ed. J. E. Benton. Gainesville: University of Florida Press.

Ward, Stephen, and Rachel Gibson. 2003. "On-Line and on Message? Candidate Websites in the 2001 General Election." *British Journal of Politics and International Relations* 5 (2): 188–205.

Ward, Stephen, Rachel Gibson, and Wainer Lusoli. 2003. "Online Participation and Mobilization in Britain: Hype, Hope and Reality." *Parliamentary Affairs* 56 (4): 652–88.

Weaver, David, and Dan Drew. 1993. "Voter Learning in the 1990 Off-Year Election: Did the Media Matter?" *Journalism Quarterly* 70 (2): 356–68.

Weaver, David, and Dan Drew. 1995. "Voter Learning in the 1992 Presidential Election: Did the 'Nontraditional' Media and Debates Matter?" *Journalism and Mass Communication Quarterly* 72 (1): 7–17.

Weaver, David, and Dan Drew. 2001. "Voter Learning and Interest in the 2000 Presidential Election: Did the Media Matter?" *Journalism and Mass Communication Quarterly* 78 (4): 787–98.

Webster, James G., and Patricia F. Phalen. 1997. *The Mass Audience: Rediscovering the Dominant Model.* Mahwah, NJ: Lawrence Erlbaum.

Welch, Susan, and John R. Hibbing. 1997. "The Effects of Charges of Corruption on Voting Behavior in Congressional Elections, 1982–1990." *Journal of Politics* 59 (1): 226–39.

Welch, William P. 1982. "Campaign Contributions and Legislative Voting: Milk Money and Dairy Price Supports." *Western Political Quarterly* 35 (4): 478–95.

Western, Bruce, and Simon Jackman. 1994. "Bayesian Inference for Comparative Research." *American Political Science Review* 88 (2): 412–23.

Wilhelm, Anthony G. 2000. *Democracy in the Digital Age: Challenges to Political Life in Cyberspace.* New York: Routledge.

Williams, Paul, and John C. Tedesco. 2006. *The Internet Election: Perspectives on the Web in Campaign 2004.* Lanham, MD: Rowman & Littlefield.

Wojcieszak, Magdalena. 2006. "Does Online Selectivity Create a Threat to Deliberative Democracy: Cyber Skepticism Reconsidered." *International Journal of Technology, Knowledge and Society* 1 (5): 165–74.

Wolfinger, Raymond E., and Stephen J. Rosenstone. 1980. *Who Votes?* New Haven, CT: Yale University Press.

Zaller, John, and Stanley Feldman. 1992. "A Simple Theory of the Survey Response: Answering Questions versus Revealing Preferences." *American Journal of Political Science* 36 (3): 579–616.

Zaller, John. 1992. *The Nature and Origins of Mass Opinion.* New York: Cambridge University Press.

Zhao, Xinshu, and Glen L. Bleske. 1995. "Measurement Effects in Comparing Voter Learning from Television News and Campaign Advertisements." *Journalism and Mass Communication Quarterly* 72 (1): 72–83.

Index

About the Authors

Jason Gainous is assistant professor at the University of Louisville. His research on the Internet and politics, public opinion, political behavior, and the media and politics has been published in journals such as *Political Research Quarterly, American Politics Research, Journal of Legislative Studies,* and *Political Communication,* among others.

Kevin Wagner is assistant professor and associate director of the Jack Miller Forum at Florida Atlantic University. His work focuses on political change and has been published in journals and law reviews including the *Willamette Law Review, American Review of Politics, Journal of Legislative Studies,* and *Politics and Policy.*